SERMONS
FROM THE
MYSTERY
BOX

As told by
R. Douglas Reinard

Compiled by
Cynthia L. LaRusch

Abingdon Press

Sermons from the Mystery Box

Copyright © 1991 by Abingdon Press

This book is printed on recycled acid-free paper.

ISBN 0-687-37534-7

Scripture quotations, unless otherwise noted, are from the *Holy Bible: New International Version.* Copyright © 1973, 1978, 1984 by the International Bible Society. Used by permission of Zondervan Bible Publishers.

Those noted NKJV are from The New King James Version. Copyright © 1979, 1980, 1982, Thomas Nelson Inc., Publishers.

96 97 98 99 00 01 02 03 04 — 10 9 8 7 6

MANUFACTURED IN THE UNITED STATES OF AMERICA

We dedicate this book
to our childhood Sunday school teachers,
who taught us the simple truths of Jesus
and by word and example introduced
us to God's love

ACKNOWLEDGMENTS

I would like to acknowledge my wife, Karen, who originally conceived the idea of this book. I thank her for constantly encouraging me to be what God wants me to be.

We express our gratitude to Ellen Guild, who counseled, urged, pushed, encouraged, and prodded us until this project was finished. We also thank her for typing the manuscript for this book.

ABOUT THE AUTHORS

The Reverend R. Douglas Reinard was born in Aliquippa, Pennsylvania. He attended Sterling College, Sterling, Kansas, where he graduated with a B.A. degree in Bible and Philosophy. He attended seminary at Eastern Baptist Theological Seminary, Philadelphia, Pennsylvania, where he graduated with a M.Div.

He has been a minister for fifteen years, presently serving as pastor of the North Warren Presbyterian Church in North Warren, Pennsylvania.

He resides in North Warren with his wife, Karen, and their two sons, Aaron and Jeremie.

Cynthia L. LaRusch was born in Jamestown, New York. She is a Sunday school teacher and actively involved in the Reverend Reinard's congregation. She has worked with him to compile the sermons for the book. She is also working on a novel of her own.

She lives in Warren with her husband, James, and their two children, Jamie Ann and Greg.

CONTENTS

INTRODUCTION

After graduating from seminary, the Reverend Reinard was shocked into the reality of preparing a children's sermon weekly. With the advice of one of his college professors, he began using objects that the children could relate to, in the hope that they would recall what was said at a later date. His only problem was deciding what should be used.

The answer to his question came to him when his ballpoint pen stopped working. Here was an object the children could relate to. He turned the pen's failure to work for him into a children's sermon. From that point on, he has continued the children's sermons with only a few changes.

At first he prepared weekly children's sermons with an object of his choosing. Six years later, he was challenged by a friend to let the children bring in an object of their own choosing. The object was put into an empty shoe box and concealed until it was time for the children's sermon. The only rules established in regard to the box were that nothing alive or dead could be put in the box.

It's not always easy to keep the interest of young children and still maintain discipline. Since they are very unpredictable, how they will react to a given situation is never assured. The children of Pastor Reinard's congregation are no different from any others. It is always a challenge for him to hold their interest long enough to teach them a lesson each week.

So it was when a six-year-old girl brought in the ''mystery box.'' She was excited to have been given the opportunity to put one of her treasures in the box. Throughout the week she thought hard, as she wanted an object that would really puzzle Pastor Reinard. When her father gave her a golf ball that was cracked in half, she knew that she had found the ideal object.

She was fascinated with the golf ball and eager to hear what lesson could be taught from this unusual object. Unfortunately, when Sunday arrived and the box was opened, she was not the only one fascinated with the golf ball. The children became noisy and unruly, making it almost impossible for Pastor Reinard to continue. Repeated warnings didn't seem to help. Against all odds, however, Pastor Reinard continued with the children's sermon.

An unhappy young lady took her seat. The lesson had not gone the way she had anticipated. She talked with her mother about what had happened and began to realize that she was not the only one who was disappointed at how the lesson had gone. Both she and her mother agreed that Pastor Reinard was probably feeling bad because of the way the lesson had gone. It was the young girl's decision to seek him out after the service and give him a big bear hug.

The tension and disappointment seemed to drain from Pastor Reinard's face as she poured out her heart to him. In the end, the lesson was more successful than anticipated. A lesson in love was learned that morning.

The children look forward to their special time each week. Not only are they eager to bring in an object of their own choosing, but they also are filled with excited anticipation when it comes to finding out what another child has placed in the mystery box.

Several times Pastor Reinard has tried to convince the children to let him sneak a peek at the contents of the box. However, no one has yet given in to the temptation to let him see what they have brought in.

In order to be fair to all children when the mystery box is handed out each Sunday, Pastor Reinard draws from his pocket a piece of paper that has a child's name written on it.

Before giving the mystery box out one Sunday, Pastor Reinard asked whether anyone knew why he gave the box out every Sunday. One child responded by saying that Pastor Reinard wanted them to bring something to church every week. He told all of them that was only part of the reason. He also wanted them to know that they were very special to God and to him, and so he felt they deserved a special time during the worship service.

The lessons in this book are not meant to be used exactly as they are written. They are only samples for you to bend and shape and fit into your own situations and availability of materials. Consider them to be teasers to get your imagination working to create an atmosphere of sharing and learning for both you and the children.

The true purpose of this book is to convince you that you can create a special time and place that will have eternal meaning for any child. There is nothing too wild or too mild. Just be yourself and have fun with the gospel of Jesus Christ, and you will find that the children will remember what you have taught.

Cynthia LaRusch

JESUS—GOD'S GREATEST GIFT TO US

MYSTERY BOX OBJECT: Christmas ornaments.

THEME: Jesus is God's gift to us. We can celebrate Christmas any day of the year.

SCRIPTURE: And we have seen and testify that the Father has sent his Son to be the Savior of the world. If anyone acknowledges that Jesus is the Son of God, God lives in him and he in God. And so we know and rely on the love God has for us. (I John 4:14-16)

LESSON:

Everyone is crowded around, anxiously waiting for me to open the box. These ornaments are beautiful. Let's unwrap the box very carefully. Look at all the tissue inside. Someone must have thought I was going to have a runny nose. That was thoughtful for someone to bring me tissues.

Christmas tree ornaments. (Comment on the ornaments, as follows.) This one looks like a girl driving a train. It's not a girl? You are right, it's a boy driving a train. Here is a girl sitting in a rocking chair. These are Christmas ornaments, and it's not even autumn yet.

We all know what Christmas is all about. When you put your Christmas tree up, do you put ornaments on it? Have you ever made any of them yourself? On our tree we have all kinds of ornaments. Some of the nicest ones we have are the ones we made ourselves. To make one that looks like one of these would take a long time and a lot of effort. When you get older, you will enjoy the Christmas ornaments you made yourself. They are always nice things to remember.

Why do we put ornaments on a tree? Yes, instead of having just a plain tree, we put pretty things on it to decorate it. To tell you the truth, I wouldn't mind one bit having a plain tree in my house in the winter. It would be nice to see the green when everything else is white. But when Christmas comes we add decorations to our tree to make it festive.

We can celebrate Christmas anytime, anywhere. We don't need to have a tree. We don't even need snow; Christmas doesn't depend on the weather. We can celebrate Christmas right now in this warm month. We don't even need a tree or these beautiful ornaments.

Christmas isn't just a time to give and get presents. It is the day we celebrate the birth of Jesus Christ. When we think about how much God loves us and how God sent God's only Son to be here on earth with us, that's cause for great celebration. That's the best gift God could ever give us. We can celebrate that anytime.

Remember that Jesus came to this earth as a baby, but he grew up to be a man. As a man he died on the cross for our sins, and when they put him in the tomb, he arose from the dead. Because of that we have eternal life. That means that when our life here on earth is over and our bodies die, our souls will live on and be with God in heaven.

Maybe it's too early to think about Christmas—then again, maybe it's not. We should think about Christmas and the wonder of God's coming down to earth in the form of a baby, every day of the year.

PRAYER: Father, we thank you that we can celebrate Christmas every day of the year. We are glad that there is a big celebration in December to remember Jesus' birthday and to think and reflect on why he came. But it's great to think about that each day. Help us all, both young and old, to remember to celebrate the love and goodness and mercy you showed to us by providing your Son, Jesus. In his name we pray. Amen.

GOD'S RULES ARE THE MOST IMPORTANT

MYSTERY BOX OBJECT: a toy airplane.

THEME: We need rules. God has given us his laws to follow so we don't get into trouble.

SCRIPTURE: Follow my example, as I follow the example of Christ. (I Corinthians 11:1)

LESSON:

Do you know what this is? Don't you have a couple of these parked in your garage? You don't? You are way behind the times if you don't have a couple of airplanes in your garage! I'm just joking. We put a car in the garage and park airplanes in a hangar. How many of you have ever flown on a real airplane? I love to fly. It's so neat up there. The only problem is that my arms get really tired. Can you fly? No! No matter how hard we flap our arms, we will never be able to fly.

God didn't give us wings, but if we use the laws of aerodynamics properly, we can make a heavy metal plane fly up in the air. That's really something. It shows us one important thing: When we don't follow God's laws, we can't fly. When we do follow God's laws, everything is possible.

We can't fly because our bodies aren't built for it. That is not part of God's laws. If we don't follow God's laws, we will get into trouble. If we do follow God's laws, we will end up learning and will become better people. So, you see, no matter what the laws are—whether the law of God or the law that stops a car at a stop sign or the laws that teach us the difference between good and bad—if we follow them, we can never go wrong.

God's laws are more important than the laws we must obey here on earth. God tells us that if we believe in his Son, Jesus, then God will set us free from what makes us want to do bad things and get us into trouble. Isn't that neat? To be set free? We can be free, but we need to follow God's laws.

Every time you see an airplane up in the air, maybe you can think about the reason it is up there—because the builder of that airplane and the person flying it are obeying God's laws of aerodynamics. We need to follow all of God's laws.

PRAYER: Lord, we thank you for laws that keep our universe from total destruction. We want to thank you also for all of your laws, which teach us to live the way we should live. Teach us more about your laws. In Jesus' name we pray. Amen.

GOD PLANNED THAT WE SHOULD EAT MANY NUTRITIONAL FOODS

MYSTERY BOX OBJECT: a toy koala bear.

THEME: We should not pig-out on just one type of food, but we should eat many different foods in order to have a balanced diet.

SCRIPTURE: As God has said: "I will live with them and walk among them, and I will be their God, and they will be my people." (II Corinthians 6:16*b*)

LESSON:

Oh! Look at this. I have a cute little kitten in the box today. It's not a kitten? Yes, you are right. It's a koala bear! We call them koala bears, but did you know they are not really bears? But they do look like bears; in fact, this one looks just like a teddy bear, doesn't it?

Do any of you have a real pet koala at home? No? Do any of you know where koalas live? Not in Africa or in the woods near here. Do they live in the jungle? Well, some of the koalas live a long way from civilization, and some live very near towns. I'm not an expert source on koala bears, but I think they live on the continent of Australia, which is on the other side of the world. So it's doubtful that any of us will run into a koala in our backyard.

Koalas are cute, aren't they? They like to eat only one thing. I like to eat a lot of different things. Sometimes I like a piece of fish and other times I might like a pizza, and other times I might like a chicken leg and corn on the cob. They all taste good to me. But koalas like one thing to eat: eucalyptus leaves. That's all they want to eat, and that can create a problem. I read a report in a magazine recently that claimed that Australia is running out of eucalyptus trees because the koalas are stripping them clean of leaves, causing the trees to die. What will the koalas eat when there are no more eucalyptus leaves? That's right. The koalas won't eat anything else. That means we must plant more trees and control the koalas so they won't all die.

The problem of the koalas should remind us that it's a good idea for us to eat various foods. Now, I realize that not everyone likes liver or spinach, but there are many things we should eat that are good for us—whether we like them or not. If we ate only ice cream every day, pretty soon the world would run out of ice cream. We all would be pretty sick, too. Koalas are different from us, because they never get sick from just eating eucalyptus leaves. God planned for us to eat many different foods. The rule in our house is that we have to try everything at least once. That doesn't mean that we have to like it, but we do have to try it. Sometimes we have found that people in our house learned to like things they didn't think they liked! The next time they said it tasted a little better. So we should always try new foods.

Remember, the tendency will be to go home today and eat a lot of candy. Make sure you eat a lot of good nutritional foods and just one piece of candy.

PRAYER: Father, we want to thank you for the variety of foods you have given us as a balanced diet. Help us to remember this week, as we sit down and eat the food that has been prepared for us, not to complain about something we don't like, but to just give it a try. We might just like it. Amen.

WHEN WE ALL WORK TOGETHER, HOW HAPPY WE'LL BE

MYSTERY BOX OBJECT: several small boxes, one inside the other; in the last box is one little pop-bead.

THEME: The Lord has put us all together as a church family to do exciting things.

SCRIPTURE: If you can do anything, take pity on us and help us. (Mark 9:22*b*)

LESSON:

Oh my! Have any of you opened a gift like this? You've never received one? Then you never know how exciting life can really be! I knew it would be just a matter of time before something like this happened. Do you want me to tear off the paper? You're anxious to see what's inside, aren't you? I think that's why this mystery box object is wrapped up in all these boxes—to make me work for it and be anxious to find out what is inside the last box.

We've finally reached the end! Does anyone know what this is? Yes, it's a pop-bead. You didn't think I knew that because I am so old, right?

This is just one bead. I can't put it around my neck; it doesn't fit. It's just one bead. What am I going to do with it? I have an idea. I'll put it on my tie. But the tie doesn't have any holes for me to put the pop-bead through, and so it won't stay. We need a whole lot of beads to make something nice.

If I had received only one box this morning instead of several, it wouldn't have been quite as exciting. As we kept opening the boxes, it got more and more exciting. It was probably exciting for the wrapper as she or he got all these boxes together.

The church is a lot like that. The Lord put us together on purpose to do some pretty exciting things. If just one of us goes out into the world and tells other people about Jesus, that is not much of a witness, is it? But if we all go out and tell others about Jesus, then that can be pretty exciting. One bead isn't very pretty or exciting, but if you put all the beads together, then they will be very pretty, and useful too. It's the same with the boxes. Of course, it's always exciting when we open one box each Sunday morning, but when we go through six boxes to find the mystery object, that makes it even more exciting.

God has called us to be a church that works together to convince people to love Jesus. All of us together make up the church. God has promised that he will make us special and help us do exciting things for him. Isn't that neat? When you come to church, you aren't the only one there. That would be boring. But there are a lot of us, and we can have fun together and enjoy Jesus Christ together.

I want you to think about that the next time you open a present. Think about the excitement there is in being a Christian and in being together in our church as opposed to just being all alone. Let's thank God for our church.

PRAYER: Father, I want to thank you for making us exciting people. Thank you that all of us together can have fun and share the love of your Son, Jesus. Thank you for that, too. Amen.

HOW DOES GOD SPEAK TO US?

MYSTERY BOX OBJECT: Pussy willow branches.

THEME: God tells us what he wants us to do through prayer and through the Bible.

SCRIPTURE: Devote yourselves to prayer, being watchful and thankful. (Colossians 4:2)

All Scripture is God-breathed and is useful for teaching, rebuking, correcting and training in righteousness. (II Timothy 3:16)

LESSON:

I want you to know that I tried every way possible to look in the box today! The box carrier was tough and wouldn't even give me a peek or a hint!

Look, the box is covered with tissue. It's a magic trick. Ta-da! I'll give you the tissue, in case you have to blow your nose if my sermon is too sad.

Does anyone know what this is? Yes, it's a pussy willow. We have a pussy willow tree in our backyard. When do these little pussy willows grow on the bush? In the middle of winter? No! They grow in the spring. I think spring must be just around the corner. In this wintry weather, we all need to hear that.

How do we know spring is coming? Is it possible that winter will be with us for twelve more months? Let me tell you one way that I know spring is on its way. Every Thursday night we go to a basketball game. We started going to these games about a month ago, and when we would leave the house, it was dark outside. When we leave the house now, at the same time we have been leaving, the sun is still shining. The days are getting longer, and the nights are getting shorter. Pretty soon pussy willows will all be out. If you gently push back the snow in your yard, you may find tulips pushing their way up through the ground.

Isn't it great how God takes care of things? Isn't it great that you don't have to stand out in the yard and yell, "Hey, tulips, it's time to grow!"? God helps the tulips know when it's time to grow and when it's time to die back to the ground again. The trees naturally push their leaves out in the spring, and in the autumn their leaves automatically fall off. Wouldn't it be great if we all would respond to God in the same way? Just like the flowers and the trees and the birds that fly south when it gets cold, and the pussy willows. You know, it's possible. We can know and respond exactly the way God wants us to.

How can you know what God wants you to do? The easiest way to find out what God wants you to do is to read your Bible. For some of you, it may be hard, because you can't read yet, but your mom or dad might read it to you. If you know how to read, then you should read your Bible and find out what God wants you to do.

The second way to know what God wants you to do is to pray to God and ask him to show you the right things to do. Then, like the tulips and the pussy willows, you'll know exactly what God wants you to do. You won't have to just stand around and wait for someone to say, "You are supposed to do something good today!'' You'll know automatically that God wants you to do good things and how to do them.

PRAYER: Father, we thank you for pussy willows, flowers, trees, birds, and animals, which know exactly what they should do all the time. We need to understand what you want us to do. Help us, through Sunday school and church and through our parents to know and understand these things so that, like the pussy willows, we can do the right thing at the right time. Amen.

WE CAN'T SEE GOD, BUT WE STILL BELIEVE IN HIM

MYSTERY BOX OBJECT: a toy stuffed animal.

THEME: God is real, even though we can't touch him or see him.

SCRIPTURE: God is spirit, and his worshipers must worship in spirit and in truth. (John 4:24)

LESSON:

For a change, I know what is in the box. I don't always know. Look at this! It's a stuffed animal! Does anyone know what this guy is? Yes, it is a —————— (tell what kind of animal it is). We all know that stuffed animals aren't real. Are you real? Are you sure? There's one way to tell if you are real, and that is to touch yourself. Are you there? If you are, then you are real. You can reach out and touch a stuffed animal, but it's not real. It's just pretend.

At your age, it is normal to have friends who aren't real. So if you talk to your dolls and toys when you play with them, that's okay. There's nothing wrong with that. As you grow older, you will learn the difference between what's real and what's pretend. You wouldn't open a can of dog food for a toy dog, would you? You are already learning the difference between reality and make-believe.

A lot of adults stop and think about how they can't reach out and touch God, and then they think that God isn't real. Do you think God is real, even though you can't touch him? God is real. God is alive. Let's think about it in another way: Clouds are real, but you can't touch them, or at least not in the same way you can touch yourself.

God is what we call a Spirit, and so we can't actually see God or touch him, but he's still there. Adults who have learned the difference between make-believe and reality still believe in God. Those are the people who are really special. God will open their eyes and minds to see things that they wouldn't ordinarily know—things about God himself and how to live for him and how to show love toward others.

Jesus said in the Bible that those who walked with him while he was on this earth, those who touched him and saw him, were special because they believed. Those who came later, and that means you and me, who would not see him as a human being, would be even more special because they would believe without seeing and touching.

Stuffed animals are't real, but you are. So is God. Don't let anyone tell you that God is not real, that God is not alive. As you grow older, you may run into other adults who don't believe in God. They are very confused and don't believe as we do. We need to pray for them and help them to understand what they are missing.

PRAYER: Lord, I thank you that your power is great in the midst of our lives, even though we can't see you or touch you. Father, I pray that as all of these children grow older, they will feel you in the midst of their lives and know and understand that you are real and that you are with them always. Amen.

HARD WORK WILL MAKE YOU
FEEL GOOD . . . GOOD . . . GOOD

MYSTERY BOX OBJECT: Two peas in a pod.

THEME: God planned for us to work and not be lazy.

SCRIPTURE: Each one should test his own actions. Then he can take pride in himself, without comparing himself to somebody else. (Galatians 6:4)

LESSON:

This is very interesting. What is it? Two peas in a pod? Do the peas come out of the pod? Vegetables are very good for you. They come in different sizes and shapes. I have never seen little peas with faces and hands! Sometimes they come out smashed, but never quite like this. How many of you have ever shelled peas? Isn't that a lot of fun? Especially if you have a bushel to shell.

When we plant our garden in the spring, we have to plant a lot of peas. The peas we plant are the kind you open with your thumb and then push all the peas out of the center of the pod. It takes a lot of work to do that, and it's not easy. Why didn't God make peas so that all you have to do is hold a basket under a tree, shake the tree, and have all the peas fall out into the basket? That would be easier.

It takes a lot of work to put vegetables on the table. Someone has to till the soil, plant the seed, and pick the vegetables when they are grown. At harvest time, someone has to can them or freeze them. We need to think about all the work that goes into the food we eat. Most of the time we just pull the chair up to the table and eat, and we really don't think about the work that goes into the food.

God planned for us to work for the things we have. That includes our life in the church. We have to work at being Christians and always try to do better. It doesn't come easy. You're at the stage now where you are just beginning to learn and grow in Jesus. You've got a lot of work ahead of you. Don't you think it would be easier if God would snap his fingers and make us all good Christians without our having to work at it? It might be easier, but not necessarily better.

From working for what we have, we learn to appreciate it more. Vegetables taste better to me if I've had to work to grow and pick them. Growing as a Christian, being a better follower of Christ, makes me feel better as I work at it. I can look back and see how much I've grown with my work and God's help. It is much better than eating the vegetables I've grown.

Next time you eat a vegetable, think about the work it takes to be a Christian and that you are beginning that work now. Eat different kinds of vegetables, so that you will grow up with strong, healthy bodies.

PRAYER: Father, we thank you for all the good food you provide for us. Thank you for all the different vegetables. We know that it takes a lot of work to make those vegetables, and it takes a lot of work to be good Christians. Remind us, when we are tired, that you want us to work hard in everything we do. Bless us, we pray. Amen.

ONLY GOD CAN SMOOTH OUT OUR ROUGH EDGES

MYSTERY BOX OBJECT: a smooth stone.

THEME: God polishes the rough edges of our lives.

SCRIPTURE:

> He made my mouth like a sharpened sword,
>> in the shadow of his hand he hid me;
> he made me into a polished arrow
>> and concealed me in his quiver. (Isaiah 49:2)

LESSON:

Let's see what's in the box today. I'm going to open it over here next to you, in case it pops out.

Everyone knows what this is. This is a stone. I am sure you all have seen stones similar to this one. Aren't the colors in this stone pretty? It's very different, isn't it? I have a stone at my house that is all black except for one small line all the way around the center. It's different, too. We can pick up all kinds of stones, and each will be different.

A long time ago, I am sure, this stone didn't look like this. Look how smooth it is. Do you think the person who brought this stone today sanded it down so that it would be smooth? No, this is the way the person found it. Probably, water flowed over this stone for a long time, wearing the sharp, rough edges down. Now we have a nice smooth stone.

What about the colors in this stone? How do you think they appeared? I'm not a geologist, so I don't know a lot about stones, but sometime or another, when God was making this stone, a couple of different colored rocks got mixed together.

God does that to us. Sometimes God polishes us up so that we're smooth, and God paints us kind of pretty, so that we look special and unique. By studying the Bible and learning to be the way that God wants us to be, we smooth down the rough edges of our lives.

I am sure you would rather run your hand over a smooth stone, like this one, rather than over one that has rough and sharp edges. In the same way, we would rather be around other people who are nice to get along with and who are happy and pleasant. That's exactly the kind of person God wants us to be. We need to get the rough edges smoothed down, so that we're not so sneaky and nasty. And, like the beautiful colors in this stone, we need to let the unique things shine through our personalities, so everyone can see them and know that God created each of us to be special.

I imagine that you could go into any stream and pick up a stone that is particularly beautiful. But you won't find another one just like this one. Each stone is different. Maybe, if you find a small one, your mom and dad will allow you to take it home, and you can set it in your bedroom and look at it. That may remind you that you want to be smooth and colorful like that so that your special personality and uniqueness will shine through. God will help you to be the kind of person you should be.

PRAYER: Father, we thank you for giving us special things, like this stone, that we can look at and that helps to remind us of the way we should be. Help us to turn to you every day, and allow you to smooth down our nasty rough edges and turn us into the persons you want us to be. Amen.

GOD WANTS US TO OBEY

MYSTERY BOX OBJECT: a doll.

THEME: Parents say no to us because they love us.

SCRIPTURE: If you then, though you are evil, know how to give gifts to your children, how much more will your Father in heaven give the Holy Spirit to those who ask him! (Luke 11:13)

LESSON:

Let's see what's in the mystery box today. How many of you would like a doll like this? I noticed that all of the girls raised their hands, but few, if any, of the boys did. How many of you would like a toy dump truck to play with? That's strange. All the boys raised their hands, but few of the girls did. I think you're fooling me, because I happen to know a little girl who received a beautiful doll for Christmas last year, and she was more interested in playing with her cousin's dump truck than with her new doll. That's okay. I also know a boy whose bed is covered with boy dolls and stuffed animals. There's nothing wrong with that! In fact, it's a good idea to play with a variety of toys. But some toys are not good for us, and our parents won't let us have them. Has that ever happened to you? Parents protect their children from bad things.

Are there any television programs your parents won't let you watch? There are probably a lot of them. Your parents don't let you watch everything on television because there are some shows that just aren't good for you to see. Your parents are protecting you from those bad shows.

While you are growing up, there will be some things that are not good for you. As long as you live at home, your parents will try to protect you from bad things. You might think they are being mean to you. Do you ever think your parents are mean when they say, "No, you can't do that"? You may think to yourself, "I have the meanest parents in the world." Parents keep bad things away from their children because they love their children very, very much.

The next time your mom or dad says no, think about the reason why. They don't want you climbing on the roof of the house because you might fall off and get hurt. They don't want you to ride a bicycle on the main highway because you might get hit by a car. Your parents love you very much. Even more than this doll is loved, and this is a very special doll. Your parents think you are even more special, and they want to make sure you grow up into a good, caring adult. We should obey our parents, and once in a while we should thank them for loving us so much.

PRAYER: Lord, I thank you for the parents of all these children. I thank you that those parents love their children so much that they say no to them. We're glad that parents care enough to limit the things that their children can do and see and say because of their love. Father, continue to build them up with that love—the love that you give us through your Son, Jesus. Amen.

WHEN JESUS IS OUR SAVIOR, CHRISTMAS STAYS WITH US

MYSTERY BOX OBJECT: Christmas wrapping paper thrown around.

THEME: When we accept Jesus as our Savior, the meaning of Christmas stays with us.

SCRIPTURE: ''The virgin will be with child and will give birth to a son, and they will call him Immanuel''—which means, ''God with us.'' (Matthew 1:23)

What, then, shall we say in response to this? If God is for us, who can be against us? (Romans 8:31)

LESSON:

When we get all that paper gathered together, we will throw it away. First I have something I want to share with you. This is exactly what happens when we open our gifts on Christmas morning. Paper flies all over the place!

How many of you have Christmas presents at home that you haven't opened yet? You've opened all your Christmas presents, haven't you? Is Christmas over? Christmas isn't over? Well, you are right and wrong. Christmas day is over, but Christmas is never really over. Most of our wrapping paper is gone, and most of the celebration is over with, but Christmas isn't over. God gave his Son, Jesus, to be our Savior. Every day that we ask forgiveness for the things we do wrong and accept Jesus as our Savior and learn more about him is Christmas in our hearts. When we accept Jesus, that is only the beginning.

Christmas was the beginning of Jesus' life here on earth as a human being, but Christmas day isn't always the beginning for us. I can remember the day I turned my life over to let God direct me and guide me. It wasn't on Christmas day; it was at Easter. But it was a day of celebration, and the joy of Christmas was in my heart. The moment we accept Jesus as our Lord and Savior is the beginning of a new life in Jesus, and Christmas stays with us.

Let's quietly sit together and have a short prayer, thanking God for Christmas and our Christmas presents. Let's thank him that we can receive his Son as our Savior.

PRAYER: Lord, we thank you for the rustle of the paper. We thank you for the excitement of Christmas morning. We thank you for the opportunity of giving gifts. What a thrill it is to please someone else. Father, we thank you for the best gift of all gifts: your Son, Jesus. Even though, Father, we have finished celebrating Christmas day, help us to know that every day can be Christmas in our hearts if we only give our lives to you. Help us to share, especially with these very young lives you have entrusted us with, the need to commit their lives totally to you, so that Christmas will be in their hearts every day of the year. Amen.

JESUS WILL NEVER LEAVE US ALONE

MYSTERY BOX OBJECT: A tiny doll that will fit inside a small pouch or pocket.

THEME: Jesus is always with us to make us feel secure.

SCRIPTURE: God has said, ''Never will I leave you; never will I forsake you.'' (Hebrews 13:5*b*)

LESSON:

Look! A tiny doll. I like the little pocket I can put it in. Do you think you were ever small enough to fit into someone's pocket? No, you were never quite that small. We can't fit into anyone's pocket, but we all need security. Do you know what security is? A good way to put it is to say that security is when we are kept from harm and evil.

No matter what age we are, we need to know that someone loves us. Knowing that someone cares about us makes us feel good, and that is security.

The security for this little doll is its pocket. You may have a blanket that you sleep with sometimes, and when you are away from home overnight, you may want to take that blanket with you because it makes you feel good. We call that a security blanket. One of the best securities you have is when someone older than you, like your mom or dad, takes care of you. Another really neat form of security is a hug or kiss from someone who loves you.

As you get older, there will be many people who will offer you security, maybe a Sunday school teacher or a school teacher or a special friend. The Bible says that Jesus wants to be our security. He wants to keep us away from evil, and he wants us to know that he will always be around for us when we need him. He will never leave us. That's a wonderful security.

How many of you have ever been afraid? I've been afraid many times. I'm probably not afraid of the same things you are afraid of, but we are all frightened of things from time to time. Isn't it nice to know that Jesus is with us to take care of us? He loves us and will never leave us.

We don't fit into anyone's pocket, because pockets just aren't made that big. But we don't need pockets for security when we have someone's arm around us or when we are given a kiss by someone who loves us or when we know that Jesus is always around. Those things are security for us, and they make us feel good.

PRAYER: God, I want to thank you that you have given us special people here on earth to take care of us and help us feel secure. Thank you even more that when your Son died on the cross and rose again three days later, he didn't leave us alone. He promised to be with us always and help us feel love and security around us. Help us to know that security in our homes as we grow up. Amen.

YOU ARE NOT TOO SMALL TO BELONG TO JESUS

MYSTERY BOX OBJECT: a green leaf.

THEME: God made you the way you are for a special purpose.

SCRIPTURE: I praise you because I am fearfully and wonderfully made; your works are wonderful. (Psalm 139:14)

LESSON:

Look what I have in the box today. How many of you have seen green leaves on the trees lately? Most of the trees in my yard don't have any leaves on them! If they do, they're not green anymore. I pressed this leaf. I just put it in an encyclopedia and put a lot of weight on it and pressed it! It sounds like paper, but it's a leaf. I wanted to show you this leaf when I plucked it off a striped maple tree in my yard. There's something very special about it.

Look at the edges of the leaf. See the little circles that are cut? Do you think I did that with a pair of scissors? How do you think that happened? A caterpillar? No, but that's a good guess. It wasn't an ant or gypsy moths or the weather or big staples. Was it God? In a way, I guess, you could say he did it, but he did it through something else. A bee did this. It didn't sting the leaf—it ate a piece out of it. This particular bee is called a leaf-cutter bee. These bees clip out pieces of leaves and take them back to their nests. Can you imagine where their nests are? These bees don't live in a hive; they live in the ground. That's different, isn't it? You never expect to see a bee that lives in the ground and cuts pieces of leaves off trees. Really strange!

God has done some pretty wonderful things. First of all, the tree itself is different. It's called a striped maple; it has stripes running up and down the tree.

Then God sent along a bee that cuts perfect circles from leaves. I can't even cut a circle that well. Boy, oh boy, God really does some strange things. Doesn't he know that bees are supposed to live in hives? Doesn't God know that bees are supposed to go to flowers and get nectar to make honey? They're not supposed to cut pieces out of leaves!

The God whom we serve and the God we know is a great and wonderful God. He does many marvelous and miraculous things. He made every one of us and all the other creatures of the earth. Each of us and each of the other creatures are all different and unique.

As we enter the Advent season, we will begin to study the birth of Jesus, and we will be talking about the prophets, who told the story of Jesus long before he was born. God made very unique people who had a story to tell others. As we study and grow in this special Advent season, we need to understand that God planned the birth of his Son down to the tiniest detail.

Now you wouldn't think that God would have the time to worry about a bee that cuts holes in a leaf, but he does. And he has enough time to care about each one of you. God wants you to know his son, Jesus Christ. He wants you to know that Jesus was born in a manger and grew up to be a man. He came to this earth as a baby so that we could come to him and know that he loves us and understands us because he experienced all the same things that you and I experience every day.

God made you the way you are for a special purpose. He wants you to be who you are, and he wants you to know his Son so that you can follow him. You are not too small, you are not too different, and you are not too strange to know Jesus and to love him and for him to love you.

PRAYER: Father, we thank you for the special little bee that can make perfect circles in a leaf that comes from an unusual tree. We know that just as you care about that tiny bee, so also you care about us. We are glad to know that we are never too small to belong to you and that you love us just as we are right now. Bless us in the week ahead and remind us of your love and your special plan for our lives. Amen.

THIS IS MY FATHER'S WORLD

MYSTERY BOX OBJECT: a starfish.

THEME: God is in control of everything around us.

SCRIPTURE:

The king's heart is in the hand of the LORD;
he directs it like a watercourse
wherever he pleases. (Proverbs 21:1)

LESSON:

How many of you have ever been to the seashore and found a starfish? That's a fun thing to do, walk along the beach and look for starfish. A starfish is one of God's unique creatures.

If this starfish were alive, and we were to cut off one of its arms, do you know what would happen? Yes, the arm would grow back again. What if I cut off your arm? Would it grow back? No, because God made us totally different from the starfish. This is a special creature that God made. It almost looks like it belongs up in the sky instead of in the ocean.

Do you remember what was up in the sky when the wise men came to see Jesus? A star. When we think of a starfish, perhaps it can remind us of the stars in the sky. God not only created starfish and you and I, but he also created the stars. God not only takes care of the starfish and you and I, but he also takes care of the stars in the sky.

Why was the star that led the wise men to Bethlehem so bright? Because God made it that way. He has control over the stars. That's something to think about. God is in control of everything around us. We should let him take control of our lives, instead of trying to take control ourselves.

We can all see this special starfish. When the weather is good, we can go out at night and see the stars. Maybe we will be able to see some of the constellations, like the Big Dipper or the lion or one of the others. Every time we do that we should think about God. God controls the stars. He controls you and I, and he takes care of all of us. We didn't even have to ask him to take care of us, he loves us that much. Let's join together in prayer.

PRAYER: God, I want to thank you for taking care of each one of us. Very seldom have we stopped to ask you to take care of us, and yet you do it anyway. We thank you for doing that. Thank you for helping all these children to grow from little babies to young children, and soon to young adults. Lord, continue to take care of them. Continue to let them hear the word of your Son, Jesus, that they may make the choice to accept him as their Lord and Savior. I pray in the name of Jesus. Amen.

YOU ARE LOVED

MYSTERY BOX OBJECT: a stuffed animal with a shirt that has a saying on it.

THEME: There are a lot of people who love and care about you.

SCRIPTURE: Then they can train the younger women to love their husbands and children. (Titus 2:4)

LESSON:

The box is heavy this week. It doesn't rattle when I shake it. It must be full. Look at this! Can you read what the shirt says? It says, '' ———— '' (read aloud the saying on the shirt). Do any of you have shirts that say somebody loves you? If you think about it, you'll realize that there are a lot of people who love you. We could start the list with your mom and dad. There are some moments when you may think that your mom and dad don't love you. They make you brush your teeth and go to bed early, and they don't let you watch television whenever you want to. The reason they do all those things is that they love you and care what happens to you. Even your brothers and sisters love you. You might not be so sure about that sometimes, either. I bet you have grandparents that love you, too. There are so many people who love you. If we were to march around this room, there would be many, many people who would tell you they love you and are concerned about what happens to you.

For ——— (name of person who owns the teddy bear or whatever type of stuffed animal you use), it's good to know that ——— (name of stuffed animal) loves him. I'm sure that when ——— hugs this bear, it feels good to have the bear's arms around him (her). Have you ever been afraid and then received a big hug from someone? Next time you're feeling a little afraid, ask someone who loves you for a hug. That's a special way to say, ''I love you.''

One of the biggest problems in the church is that people are afraid to let other people in the church know that they are really concerned about them and really love them. We don't see very many people hugging each other in the church. That's probably one thing we need to improve. Let's all try to show each other how much we care and express it through a hug. It's important to be loved. Remember that people in church love you and, more important, God loves you. When you've had a really bad day, it always helps to make you feel better to have a hug from a friend. When there doesn't seem to be anyone around who cares, we can be thankful that we have Jesus. We can be sure that he loves us.

PRAYER: Father, we thank you that we are loved. You have provided loving, caring people around us who give us hugs and support us when we are feeling sad. Now, help us to look around for someone who needs special loving and care. Help us to reach out to that person today. Amen.

GOD HAS CONTROL OVER THINGS—WE DON'T

MYSTERY BOX OBJECT: a doll like a "Popples" doll, which has a pouch in which to "hide" the doll.

THEME: God is always there to help and protect us when things happen that we don't have any control over.

SCRIPTURE: As the mountains surround Jerusalem, so the LORD surrounds his people both now and forevermore. (Psalm 125:2)

LESSON:

What is this? It's a Popples doll! It has funny little red cheeks. Do any of you have red cheeks? When you are outside in the cold, your cheeks turn red. Can your face ever get red in the summer? Yes. We have to protect our faces from the sun with sunblock. We have to protect our bodies both in the winter and in the summer. I don't think this little guy protected its body very well.

Let's take a look at this doll. Look at that; it pops right out of its pouch! I guess that's its protection. That's pretty nifty. In the winter we wear heavy clothes, and in the summer we wear light clothes. This little doll is protected when it goes back into its pouch, like this (put doll inside pouch).

What other kinds of protection can you think of? (Respond to answer.) God protects us. God has promised to give each of us a guardian angel. What other protection is there? Animals get more fur when the weather turns cold. In the spring they lose most of it, because they don't need their protection in warm weather. Name one thing that protects you in your home. (Respond to answer.) A smoke alarm helps us to know when there may be a fire in our house. We should also have a fire extinguisher, just in case we need it.

There is a better kind of protection at home, and that's the protection you get from your parents. Have you ever been afraid of the dark? I used to be when I was younger. I wasn't afraid when my dad was with me, because I figured that if anything jumped at us, he would take care of it. I felt protected by my mom and dad. There are two important kinds of protection. The first type is our parents. They teach us to do the right things and punish us when we do the wrong things. That's part of their protection for us. But the second, and the best, protection is God. He gives us each a guardian angel to watch over us. That doesn't mean we can do stupid or dangerous things. God expects us to use our brains and do good and wise things. Isn't it great that God is always around to help and protect us when things happen that we don't have any control over? He's our friend.

PRAYER: Lord, I thank you for letting us be here today. We thank you for watching out for all of us. Thank you for all the protection you allow us to have in our homes, not only the safety features, but also our moms and dads, who watch over us and take care of us. Continue to bless us with both kinds of protection, so that we might surely grow up to be your people and receive your Son, Jesus, as our Lord and Savior. Amen.

GOD WANTS US TO USE, NOT ABUSE, THE THINGS HE GIVES US

MYSTERY BOX OBJECT: two small rocks.

THEME: God wants us to use all the things he's given to us in good ways.

SCRIPTURE: God blessed them and said to them, "Be fruitful and increase in number; fill the earth and subdue it. Rule over the fish of the sea and the birds of the air and over every living creature that moves on the ground."

Then God said, "I give you every seed-bearing plant on the face of the whole earth and every tree that has fruit with seed in it. They will be yours for food. And to all the beasts of the earth and all the birds of the air and all the creatures that move on the ground—everything that has the breath of life in it—I give every green plant for food." And it was so. (Genesis 1:28-30)

LESSON:

Does anyone know what this is? It's a rock. Look at the side of it. Someone has obviously used this rock. Look how round the hole is. This one looks like it is well worn and used, too. Have you ever used rocks or stones for anything besides throwing? What do you use rocks for? We can take large rocks and build a wall. It would take a lot of stones this size to make a wall, wouldn't it? We'd need some bigger ones, too. What else do we use rocks and stones for? (Respond to answers.) We can grind two pieces of stone together to get sand.

Rocks and stones can be used in many different ways. When I was in college, I walked through a farmer's field and kicked a stone, but it didn't move. I thought my foot was going to fall off, though. When I dug the stone out of the ground, I found that it was quite large and round. It was broken in half. There was another piece to it, but I couldn't find it. Someone had used that stone before I found it. Can you guess who could have used it? Maybe it was a stone that the Indians had used to rub back and forth on a larger stone to grind corn. I was lucky to find it. I have it at my house, and someday I'll show it to you.

Stones can also be very destructive. What do you think the people in the church would say if I took this stone and threw it at the big window in the back of the church? They wouldn't be very happy, especially since we spent a lot of money to get those windows fixed. Throwing stones isn't a good thing to do, but there are many good things we can do with them.

We can use everything God has given us in very good ways, or we can use them in bad ways. Now, how do you think God would rather have us use the things he has given us? Of course, in the good way. Maybe the next time you pick up a stone and want to throw it, you will think about what God intended that stone to do. I am sure you will not throw it, because God would never want us to throw stones at people. When you pick up a stick and are ready to hit someone with it, remember the reason God made that stick. He made sticks for campfires or to stake up tomato plants or something like that. God wants us to use all the things he has given us, including stones, in good ways.

PRAYER: Lord, you have given us so many things that are useful to us in our everyday lives. Help us to use the resources you have given us wisely and not foolishly. Help us not to abuse them but to use them for our good. Thank you for all the good and useful things you have given us. Amen.

IF YOU ARE FEELING SAD, YOU CAN CHANGE YOUR OUTLOOK

MYSTERY BOX OBJECT: a toy snake.

THEME: When we're feeling sad, we should think of all the good things in our lives. That will help us to change our outlook on life.

SCRIPTURE: Finally, brothers, whatever is true, whatever is noble, whatever is right, whatever is pure, whatever is lovely, whatever is admirable—if anything is excellent or praiseworthy—think about such things. (Philippians 4:8)

LESSON:

I'm going to get out of here—snakes! Of all the things in the world that I don't like, snakes are number one on the list. I can put up with with mud. I can put up with cats. I can even put up with spiders, but I don't like snakes.

We all have something that we don't like. Is there something that you don't like? Maybe it's food. Can you think of some food you don't like? I can think of one. I don't like beets. Maybe you don't like a particular kind of weather. Some people don't like snow; some people don't like rain; some people don't like sunshine. There is always something that someone doesn't like. If we think about all of the things that we don't like, we can sure think of a lot of nasty things, can't we? I can think of liver and onions, snakes, and, oh, I could just go on and on with all the yucky, nasty things I don't like. Couldn't you do that? But, you know, if we kept thinking about the things that we don't like, pretty soon, we would get to feeling really bad. That's not what God wants us to do.

God wants us to think about the good things. He wants us to think about what he's doing for us. Instead of standing here and thinking about all the things I don't like, I'm going to change! I'm going to start thinking about all the good food that I eat, and I'm going to think about all the warm clothes that I have to wear, and I'm going to think about the boots I have that will keep my feet dry and warm.

When I think about all the people who care about me and love me, I feel good. You know, if we think about all the good things we have, instead of thinking of the bad things, we can change our whole outlook on life. How many of you have gotten up in the morning in a bad mood? Come on, admit it. I did when I was your age. I'd get up—and I didn't want to get out of bed—and I was nasty. My mother would tell me to wear a certain shirt, and I would say, "I don't want to wear that shirt, it's ugly!" And sometimes I would go to school, and I would be nasty, and the teacher would tell me to sit down. That would make me even angrier, because I didn't want to sit down. Then the teacher would tell me there was work to be done, and I would want to go to sleep. Did you ever have a day start out like that and then just keep getting worse and worse all day long? It might be a good idea, when you have a day starting out wrong, to thank the Lord that you even woke up and that you are alive and that you have food to eat for breakfast and clothes to wear. If you can change your thinking, you will change your whole day.

Let's think more about the things we do like. It will make a big difference in the way other people will see us, and it will make a difference in the way we treat other people.

PRAYER: Lord, we thank you that with your help we are able to make changes for the better. Remind us when we are feeling sad to think of all the good things that surround us, which you have given to us. Help us to be thankful always. Amen.

GOD WANTS US TO LOOK OUR BEST

MYSTERY BOX OBJECT: a comb and a brush.

THEME: God has given us things to take care of ourselves with, so we can stay healthy and look our best.

SCRIPTURE: Then David got up from the ground. After he had washed, put on lotions and changed his clothes, he went into the house of the LORD and worshiped. Then he went to his own house, and at his request they served him food, and he ate. (II Samuel 12:20)

LESSON:

Everyone knows what these are! A brush and comb for our hair. They are used to take care of our hair. How many of you like to comb your hair? When your mom says, "Go comb your hair," do you just go and do it without complaining? That never happened when I was growing up. My mother would always tell me to comb my hair, and I would do this (use fingers on hair for comb).

Why do we even comb our hair? We look better when we comb our hair, don't we? Did you ever look at yourself first thing in the morning before you had a chance to comb your hair? Wow! I always look like some kind of scary monster. That's why we comb our hair—to look our best.

There are other things we do to make ourselves look better. We wash our hands and faces, which helps us to stay clean and healthy. Your hair will stay healthy if you brush it regularly, too, instead of letting it fly around like a bunch of weeds.

God has given us things to use so that we can stay healthy. There are other things we need to take care of besides our hair and our bodies, and they are our family and our friends. We need to make sure that they are treated well by others around us. And, of course, we should treat each other very well and love each other. That's a good way to take care of each other. Let's bow our heads and quietly thank Jesus for loving us and for giving us friends and families to love.

PRAYER: Father, I thank you that you've given us responsibilities as young children to take care of ourselves. I thank you also, Lord, that you have given us moms and dads, brothers and sisters, husbands and wives, so that we can love them and take care of them, too. Help us to understand in some small way how important they are to us. When things aren't going so well at home, help us to know how valuable these loved ones are. Give us the opportunity to give them a hug and tell them we love them. Amen.

GOD WILL HELP US WITH OUR PROBLEMS

MYSTERY BOX OBJECT: a microscope or a magnifying glass.

THEME: Sometimes we magnify our problems, making them bigger than they are.

SCRIPTURE: According to my earnest expectation and hope that in nothing I shall be ashamed, but that with all boldness, as always, so now also Christ will be magnified in my body, whether by life or by death. (Philippians 1:20 NKJV)

LESSON:

As you all can see, this is a microscope. What can you see through a microscope? You can see little, tiny things through the microscope, which makes those little things look larger. What is the name of the instrument that helps us see things far away? It's called a telescope. So we use a microscope to help us see tiny things and a telescope to help us see things far away.

Why do you think God made things so far away from us or so small? Wouldn't it be better if everything were the same size? Can you imagine ants that were as big as you are? The same goes for objects that are far away. God is pretty smart. He made small things and big things and things that are very close to us and things that are far away. Our eyes can't see little things that are far away, and our eyes can't see clearly tiny things up close, so God made a way for us to see them clearly. He also gives us knowledge, so that we will know how to use these instruments.

Sometimes we magnify our problems, making them bigger than they really are. We spill milk or have trouble in school or even get angry at our parents. Then we think about these problems, and as we think, the problems seem to get bigger and bigger, and we get more and more upset. We magnify them; we make them bigger than they really are. Did you ever do that? Sometimes we have to try not to act like a microscope and remember that our problems are not as big as they seem. We need to ask God to help us see things as they really are. We need to just clean up the spilled milk or try harder in school or stop being angry and forgive our parents. We need to realize that the world won't come to an end just because we have problems. God wants us to see the world and ourselves as they really are, and he will help us deal with each situation as it comes along.

PRAYER: Lord, I pray that you'll help us to see that our problems aren't as big as we sometimes think they are. Sometimes when we are little and even sometimes when we are older, we find it hard not to magnify our problems. We pray that you will help us, when we have a problem, not to enlarge it, but to deal with it and realize that it's not the end of the world. With your help, we know we can work out any problem we may have. Amen.

ONLY JESUS CAN REALLY CHANGE US

MYSTERY BOX OBJECT: an Air Force flight suit (any uniform may be used).

THEME: You can change your outside appearance and not really change at all. Only Jesus can really change us.

SCRIPTURE: Get rid of the old yeast that you may be a new batch without yeast—as you really are. For Christ, our Passover lamb, has been sacrificed. (I Corinthians 5:7)

LESSON:

(Place the uniform in a bag instead of in the box.) You'll never guess what is in the mystery box this morning. Well, actually, it's not in the box. It wouldn't fit. It's in this bag. I'll give you a hint. I have something in this bag that will make me a brand-new person. I've wanted to be someone different for many years. I can imagine that there are times you would like to be a new person, too. Did you ever feel that way? Maybe you wish you could make fewer mistakes. Maybe you have done something bad that you wish could be changed or that you could forget.

Well, the answer to all of our problems is in this bag. We can all be someone new with the old bad things gone—gone forever. I hope this works. What I have is a (name type of uniform). I'll put it on, and you will see the new me (put on the uniform).

What do you think? Here I am. This is the new me. I won't be like I used to be, now that I have the new me on.

You don't believe that? Well, you're right when you say I haven't changed. I may look different on the outside, but I'm still the same old me underneath all these clothes. Just by putting on this uniform, I haven't become new. I could color my hair purple; I could grow a beard; I could wear different clothes, even make new friends, but I would still be the same old me.

But there is hope. Paul tells us in II Corinthians that when we accept Jesus as our Savior and Lord we become a new creation. God actually makes us new. Oh, we still look the same on the outside, but God makes us brand new on the inside. He changes us. He gives us hearts of love and the desire to be like Jesus. We can start over and leave all the old bad things behind, because Jesus forgives us of those things and throws them all away. God changes us to go ahead with our lives and begin to do good things.

You can change on the outside and not really change on the inside at all. The most important change we can ever make is to accept Jesus and have God change us on the inside, where it counts.

PRAYER: Father, we want to thank you that you can help us to make needed changes in our lives. If we come to you and confess our sins and accept Jesus as our Savior, then you will change us on the inside. Help us as we learn to do good things that can only be done with your love in our hearts. In Jesus' name we pray. Amen.

WHEN YOU ARE AFRAID, REMEMBER JESUS IS WITH YOU

MYSTERY BOX OBJECT: a rubber snake.

THEME: There is no need to be afraid.

SCRIPTURE: God has said,
"Never will I leave you;
never will I forsake you."
So we say with confidence,
"The Lord is my helper; I will not be
afraid.
What can man do to me?" (Hebrews 13:5*b*-6)

LESSON:

The rule is that we can have nothing dead or alive in the box, but I never said anything about rubber replicas, did I? Do any of you have a rubber snake at home like this one? What do you do with it? You put it around your neck and pretend it's real. What else? Many times we use something like this rubber snake to scare people. My mother is deathly afraid of snakes, and my sons just love to get their grandmother. And every time, she'll run screaming, even if it is from a little rubber snake. Are any of you afraid of real snakes? Go ahead, admit it. I will—I don't like snakes. Why are we afraid of snakes? They bite. Has anyone here ever been bitten by a snake? Have any of you ever seen a python? They're very big, let me tell you. Most snakes can't take much of a bite out of you. But it's the poisonous one you've got to worry about biting you. Why else are you afraid of snakes? I just don't like those slimy looking creatures crawling through the grass. I never did like snakes.

I'm sure there other things you are afraid of. Maybe the dark. Maybe your big brother. Maybe your little sister. We can be afraid of a lot of things, can't we? Sometimes our fears are imaginary. The fears are in our minds, and are not real. For instance, if we are afraid of the dark, most of that fear is created by our imaginations working overtime. We think of all the horrible things that *could* happen or the ugly things that lurk in the dark. There is really nothing to be afraid of; it's only our imagination. Some people are afraid to go into a dark room of a house, because something in there might get them. Sometimes they are even afraid to reach around the corner and turn on the light switch really quick, because of what might pounce at them. If they would turn on the light, they would see that it's only a room—no scary monsters. Sometimes we're afraid of snakes the same way.

In the Bible, we're told in the book of Hebrews that God will never desert us or forsake us. The Lord is our helper, and we should not be afraid. God wants us to know that he is constantly with us. He wants to take all of our fears away. If we fill our minds up with thoughts of Jesus, there will be no room for fears.

I used to be afraid of snakes, and I still don't like them. But I now know that God is with me and that I don't have to be afraid of snakes. In fact, I don't have to be afraid of anything in this world, because I have a helper, and he is always with me. His name is Jesus.

PRAYER: Lord, thank you for your Son, Jesus, who is with us everywhere we go and takes care of us. Help us to always be aware that Jesus is with us and that we need never to be afraid. Amen.

PENTECOST—THE BIRTHDAY OF THE CHURCH

MYSTERY BOX OBJECT: a birthday cake decorated with a bright colored flame and candles.

THEME: Celebration of the birth of the church—Pentecost Sunday.

SCRIPTURE: When the day of Pentecost came, they were all together in one place. Suddenly a sound like the blowing of a violent wind came from heaven and filled the whole house where they were sitting. They saw what seemed to be tongues of fire that separated and came to rest on each of them. . . . Those who accepted his message were baptized, and about three thousand were added to their number that day. (Acts 2:1-3, 41)

LESSON:

Today I have something special in the mystery box. Shall we take a look? What kind of candles are these? Yes, they are birthday candles. There are many kinds of candles for many different uses. These particular candles are used on birthday cakes. We've all had a birthday cake with candles on it.

I just happen to have a cake with me that these candles go on. It's back here in another box. (Have cake ready to show children.) As you can see, this cake is decorated with a bright colored flame. There is a reason for the flame. That is a symbol of God's Spirit, which baptized those who were a part of the first church many years ago. Each year, we celebrate the beginning of the church during a special day we call Pentecost. This is a special birthday cake for a special birthday.

Let me read a few verses to you from the book of Acts, so that we can better understand what this day is all about. (Read the Scripture printed above.)

Now you can see why the cake is decorated with a flame. Let's put the candles on the cake, light them, and sing "Happy Birthday" to the church. After worship today, you can all come back up here and get a piece of this cake to take home with you. That way the birthday party of the church can go to your home with you.

PRAYER: Father, we thank you for this special day, the birthday of the church, your church. We thank you that so many years ago, you started the church with just a handful of believers. We're glad you did that and that we continue to meet in churches around the world to worship you. Help these young people, as they learn about you through this church, to always remember this special birthday—Pentecost Sunday. Amen.

GOD GAVE US A BEAUTIFUL WORLD

MYSTERY BOX OBJECT: an acorn, a leaf, green pine needles, brown pine needles, a stone, a feather, different kinds of seeds, and a pine cone.

THEME: God has given us a beautiful world for our enjoyment.

SCRIPTURE: God saw all that he had made, and it was very good. (Genesis 1:31a)

LESSON:

Wow! I guess I'll just pull all of these things out and put them on top of the box, so you can see them. These are things that are found in a playroom. Right? No? You are right! They are found outside.

Here are a pine cone and some pine needles from a pine tree. These pine needles are still green and alive, but look at these; they are brown and dead. So we have two kinds of pine needles. We also have an acorn, a stone, a feather, and some seeds. These are all kinds of things you may find outside.

How many of you like to go outside and collect different things? How many of you have ever made a leaf collection? The neat thing is that all of these things belong to God. They are unique and different, and we can learn a lot from them. These pine needles are different; yet, they both come from pine trees. We have different kinds of seeds here, too. This kind of seed blows around in the wind (hold up seed, possibly a dandelion or maple seed), and this kind falls from maple trees. These seeds come from a birch tree. God has put all of these things here for us to see and enjoy. He wants us to pick them up and touch them and learn from them. We can see that when a bird loses a feather, it grows another feather in the same place. Pine trees lose some of their needles every year, and then they grow new ones.

God has given us all of these things for us to notice and enjoy and take care of. The next time you are making a leaf collection or a stone collection, remember that God has given us all of these things for us to enjoy. Let's join together in a word of prayer.

PRAYER: God, we thank you for all of the things that you have given us. We thank you for the trees that lose their leaves and for the trees that keep their green pine needles during the winter. We thank you for all the animals that eat the little seeds and the big seeds, like some of the ones we have today. But most of all we thank you for giving us one another, because we always have one another to enjoy and rely on. You have made us so that we would be rulers over the animals. Help us to take good care of all these things you have given to us. Amen.

YOUR BODY NEEDS PLENTY OF REST

MYSTERY BOX OBJECT: a blanket.

THEME: Part of God's plan is for us to get plenty of rest.

SCRIPTURE: By the seventh day God had finished the work he had been doing; so on the seventh day he rested from all his work. (Genesis 2:2)

LESSON:

Aren't blankets nice to have? When you snuggle up in them, they feel warm and cuddly. At one time or another, all of us have had something that we enjoyed snuggling up to. Maybe it was a teddy bear or maybe it was a blanket. We all have had something that was very special to us. Going to bed isn't the same, unless you have a teddy bear or a blanket to snuggle up with.

How many of you like to go to bed? At night, when your mom and dad tell you it's time to go to bed, do you say, "Oh great! I just love to go to bed!"? Or do you say, "Oh! Do I have to go to bed?" We don't really like to go to bed, do we? We'd rather stay up and play or watch T.V.

Did you know that God has a plan for us that includes rest? When we're very young, we need more sleep, and when we get really old we need less sleep. The in-between years don't require as much sleep. Did you ever notice how much a little baby sleeps? My understanding is that children of your age need ten hours of sleep each night. So when your mom and dad tell you to go to bed, they're not trying to be mean and nasty. They want you to get your rest. In the morning, you can get up with all kinds of energy. You'll be ready to play and to go to school. The next time your mom or dad tells you to go to bed, think about that poor blanket lying on the bed, so lonesome, needing someone to sleep with! Well, that may not help. Maybe we need to remember that God's plan is for us to get plenty of rest.

Remember what the Bible says? God created the heaven and the earth and the animals and the trees and even the people. What did he do on the seventh day? He rested.

We all need rest. Even our moms and dads need rest. Not only do we need to rest at night, but also at least once a week we need to take a day off to relax and not work. Our moms and dads want you to rest so you can stay healthy. Let's think about how God wants us to rest every day, and especially that special day once a week.

PRAYER: Lord, I thank you that I don't have to stay up twenty-four hours a day. I thank you for my bed, so that I can lie down when my body and my spirit and my mind are all tired. You can give me strength and rest, so that on the next day I can do the jobs you want me to do. Bless us in your Son's name. Amen.

JESUS CHRIST IS ALIVE!

MYSTERY BOX OBJECT: a shofar (ram's horn).

THEME: Jesus wants us to celebrate his resurrection.

SCRIPTURE: Abraham looked up and there in a thicket he saw a ram caught by its horns. He went over and took the ram and sacrificed it as a burnt offering. (Genesis 22:13)

LESSON:

Everyone gather around. We had some debate today before the mystery box was brought out. A couple of boys thought there was nothing in the box. Last Easter, I took the box and brought it back empty, and we talked about the empty tomb. But there's something in the box this year!

What do you think is in the box on this Easter Sunday morning? You'll never guess. There is nothing in here that you would think has anything to do with Easter. There are no Easter rabbits, no Easter eggs, no Easter bonnet. Let me show you what is in the box.

Look at this! You think it's a powder horn? No, it's called a shofar. In the Jewish faith, in the time of Christ, a designated person would go outside the Temple and blow the shofar to let the people know it was time for a celebration or a gathering. This is a ram's horn. It sounds like this (blow horn). It doesn't sound the greatest, does it? But it is loud, and when the people heard it, they would all gather in.

We've all been called together today to celebrate. Some of you were called by your mom or dad this morning, and you didn't want to get up. Some of you were pushed to get dressed a little faster because you were going to be late. That's one way to be called. Even more important than your parents calling you and more important than the ram's horn that called people together so many years ago is God's call for us to gather together.

The scriptures tell us that on the first day of the week, which is the day we call Sunday, Christ arose from the tomb. The people who believed and who saw Jesus alive gathered on the first day of the week to celebrate the resurrection of Jesus Christ. That wasn't the day the people were used to worshiping on. They had worshiped on the last day of the week, the day we now call Saturday.

To this day, the Christians meet and celebrate on the first day of the week. So we have been called together today, not by the shofar, not by our parents, not by the leaders of this church, and not by the pastor. Jesus Christ called this meeting today. Because he rose from the dead, we are here to celebrate.

Look around at how fancy everyone looks today. Doesn't everyone look nice? We're all dressed up because we've come to celebrate the resurrection.

We will all go home to Easter bunnies, Easter eggs, big meals, and whatever else we do to celebrate Easter. If all of those things were taken away, we would still celebrate. Jesus is alive! That's what counts the most. We would still sing and praise God. He is alive! That's our call to worship.

Does anyone know who was the first person to see the risen Jesus? Yes, Mary. Now, in the Gospels there are several women named Mary, and we aren't sure which Mary it was, but we know that the first person who saw Jesus after he rose from the dead was Mary. She ran to tell the friends of Jesus.

Our job now is to tell other people that Jesus is alive. Jesus told Mary, "Go tell the disciples that Jesus is alive!" That's your job, too. Go to school and tell your friends, tell your mom and dad, tell everyone you see—Jesus is alive! People need to know that!

PRAYER: Father, I want to thank you for this first day of the week when we celebrate you. We want to thank you that your Son rose from the tomb. Bless us, so that when the Easter celebration is all over—long after the Easter eggs, the jelly beans, and the chocolate rabbits are gone—we still continue to celebrate because we know that Jesus is alive and he lives in us. Amen.

LISTEN—QUIETLY LISTEN

MYSTERY BOX OBJECT: a toy mouse wearing a hat, with its ears sticking through.

THEME: We must listen in order to hear what God is saying to us.

SCRIPTURE: Blessed is the man who listens to me, watching daily at my doors, waiting at my doorway. (Proverbs 8:34)

LESSON:

Do you like mice? This little mouse's ears are sticking through its hat. How many of you have holes in your hats? If you do have holes in your hat, they are not to stick your ears through, are they? Look at the little ears on this mouse. Have you ever really looked at anyone's ears? They are funny little things that stick on the side of our heads. You would have thought that God could have put them somewhere else so they wouldn't look so funny. Have you ever tried to picture anyone without ears? That would look funnier than ever!

What do we use our ears for? (Respond to answers.) That's right, we use our ears for listening and hearing. Let's be quiet for just a minute and hear all the sounds around us. Did you hear anything? (Respond to answers.) You should go out into your yard and just sit there for a few quiet moments. Close your eyes and listen and discover what you can hear. You may hear a bird sing or an airplane or some cars. There are a lot different sounds you can hear.

Ears are for listening, too. Now what do you think listening is? It is not only hearing, but it is putting what you hear in action as well. For example, if your mom tells you to pick up your toys, you may hear her say that, but you don't pick up your toys. You didn't really listen. That's the difference between hearing and listening.

There's a verse in the Bible that says, "All you who have ears, listen to the Word of God!" Don't just hear it; listen to it.

A mouse has a very keen sense of hearing. If a mouse doesn't hear, it just might get trampled by someone big or eaten by a bigger animal. So a mouse has to listen very well.

We need to hear, too, and listen to God's Word, so we can do what God wants us to do. God wants us to do good things. Let's bow our heads and thank God for hearing us. Let's take time to listen to him.

PRAYER: God, I thank you for giving us ears. Some of us hear so much better than others, but we still thank you for the hearing we have. Father, we ask that you would help us not only to hear, but also to listen to your Word, so that we may believe, just as the disciples. We pray that we may become disciples, too, and tell others what we have heard. Help us to understand what we hear. In Jesus' name, amen.

WE ARE MADE IN THE IMAGE OF GOD

MYSTERY BOX OBJECT: a fuzzy stuffed animal.

THEME: God created us in his own image.

SCRIPTURE: Then God said, "Let us make man in our image, in our likeness, and let them rule over the fish of the sea and the birds of the air, over the livestock, over all the earth, and over all the creatures that move along the ground." (Genesis 1:26)

LESSON:

The mystery box is all wrapped with a piece of yarn. I'm not sure whether that was to keep me out or to protect what is inside. Let's take a look.

This animal is really fuzzy, isn't it? Why don't we have as much fur as this does? That's right, we are not like animals.

Would you like to be covered with fur on a hot day? Would you like to be covered with fur on a cold day? That would probably keep us nice and warm. That's one way we are different from animals.

We can also do things that animals can't do, and you can be sure that animals can do things that we can't do. The Bible tells us that God made us in his image. That means more than just looking like God or having a form like God. We are like God in our spirit. We have a soul, and we can think and reason. No animal seems to be able to do that.

Because of the spirit that God has put in us, we can invite God's Holy Spirit to live inside us. The Holy Spirit lives inside us; he renews us and makes us different.

A cat is always a cat, and a dog is always a dog. When a dog is mean as a puppy, it will be mean as a dog. However, God gives us a chance to change. He gives us his Holy Spirit, which changes our lives and makes us even better than what we were before. That's what it means when we say we are made in the image of God. God really loves us.

PRAYER: Father, we are glad that you made us different from all the animals. We thank you for making us in your image. We invite you to live inside us to make the changes that need to be made. Amen.

GOD IS THE GREATEST INVENTOR
THERE HAS EVER BEEN

MYSTERY BOX OBJECT: pieces of cloth sewn together and a sewing machine.

THEME: God puts things together. He made this beautiful day, the sunshine, the blue sky, the white clouds, and the warm air. He's the greatest inventor there ever was.

SCRIPTURE: You alone are the LORD. You made the heavens, even the highest heavens, and all their starry host, the earth and all that is on it, the seas and all that is in them. You give life to everything, and the multitudes of heaven worship you. (Nehemiah 9:6)

LESSON:

If I'm not mistaken, this is six pieces of material sewn together. Do you like to sew? I've done a lot of sewing in my day, but I have never understood how to use a sewing machine. I've always used a needle and thread. When you're one thousand miles from home and your pants are split, you either wear them split or learn how to sew. So I learned how to sew!

Sewing is a nice hobby, and many people sew for a hobby. Sometimes it's not a hobby, but a job. Some people work in factories and make clothes.

Do any of you know how people sewed many years ago? Sewing wasn't done by machines. It was all done by hand. That takes a lot longer and is much harder to do. We have machines now that help us. You can take pieces of material, like these, and sew them together. That's how your clothes are made. Look at your clothes. Can you see a seam where the material was sewn together? At one time what you are wearing was just one large piece of cloth. Someone had to cut it to a certain size by using a pattern, and then someone sewed it together.

Let's think about a sewing machine. Someone who was very skillful put all the pieces together so the sewing machine would run. Do you think you could do that? Sometimes I scratch my head when I look at machines. Not just a sewing machine, but any machine. I wonder who knew how to put all those pieces together, so the machine would do what it is supposed to do.

Did you know that God is smarter than any person who can put together a machine? God put all the things together in the whole universe. If you think it's tough to put together a sewing machine, can you imagine how hard it is to make a tree or a whole hillside or a planet or an animal? Do you think you could make a hillside? God made all that we can see. He made you and me, and we're better than any machine that someone has made.

It's nice to have machines that help us. It's good to learn new hobbies and new skills. But maybe the next time you look at a sewing machine or a car or any machine, you will remember that we have a great God who loves us and is the greatest inventor of all. I think it would be a good idea for us to thank God for this beautiful day, which we didn't make—God did.

PRAYER: Father, you are greater than any inventor there has ever been. We thank you for sewing machines and other things you have allowed us to have. Thank you most of all for what you have created, including this beautiful day. Thank you for the sunshine, the blue sky, the white clouds, the warm air, and for friends to enjoy them with. You have truly blessed us and given us your very best. We love you. Amen.

GOD CAN CHANGE US FROM PLAIN TO BEAUTIFUL

MYSTERY BOX OBJECT: a ribbon that pulls into a bow.

THEME: God can do something special for us on the inside that we can't do for ourselves.

SCRIPTURE:
The Lord is my strength and my shield;
  my heart trusts in him, and I am helped.
My heart leaps for joy
  and I will give thanks to him in song. (Psalm 28:7)

LESSON:
Here is something very interesting. What is it? Well, it looks like a ribbon. But look (pull the ribbon), it's a bow! (Pull ribbon again.) Now it looks like a regular ribbon again.

The trick is that there are actually two ribbons. There is a smaller ribbon inside, and a larger one on the outside. It's fixed in such a way that when I pull the smaller one, it just bunches up and makes a bow.

Sometimes people think we are weird because we come to church and call ourselves Christians. As Christians, we're a lot like this bow. We have an outside part that everyone sees and that we see when we look in the mirror. We also have an inside part, called our soul or our spirit. When we allow God to pull the ribbon of our heart, we can come out to be a pretty bow, by giving our lives to Jesus. It's a possibility that the rest of the world will think we are kind of weird. That's okay. We know that God can do something special for us that we can't do for ourselves. That's the neat thing about being a Christian. We're stuck with what we see on the outside when we look in the mirror, but God can change us in such a way that we become beautiful people on the inside, where it counts. God can change us from something plain into something beautiful. I want you to think about that.

You may go on vacation this year, and you'll probably see a lot of people who don't know who you are. They don't know the bad things or the good things that you do. But you can show them you have something special in your life by letting God direct the way you act around other people. Maybe they'll see the beautiful you instead of the plain everyday you. They'll see that you have something special in your life that they may not have, and then you can tell them about Jesus and how he makes you beautiful.

PRAYER: Lord, I thank you that you can help others to see in us that which we can't put inside of ourselves. Help others to see you through each of us by the way we act and through the way we serve you. Father, bless us and help us to be a blessing. Amen.

GOD WANTS US TO ASK HIM FOR WISDOM

MYSTERY BOX OBJECT: a picture of a cat or tiger or other member of the cat family carrying its baby in its mouth.

THEME: We need to ask God to help us to be wise as we grow up and to show us how to take care of animals, insects, and plants.

SCRIPTURE: If any of you lacks wisdom, he should ask God, who gives generously to all without finding fault, and it will be given to him. (James 1:5)

LESSON:

How many of you have ever seen people carrying their babies in their mouths? People don't carry babies like that. Have you ever seen a cat, or an animal in the cat family such as this animal, carry its baby in its mouth? They do. Animals don't have hands as you and I do, so they can't pick their babies up with their arms and rock them. If they have to move their young for protection or some other reason, they pick it up with their mouth. Do you think that would hurt? Well, for us it probably would hurt. But for animals in the cat family, the mother knows exactly how to pick up the baby so that she doesn't hurt the baby.

God has so many wonderful things in this world that seem odd to us human beings. He has provided all of these things for special purposes. One of the things that we may think is a little weird is a cat picking up her baby with her mouth.

Can you think of anything else that is kind of weird? Something that an animal may do that people don't do? (Respond to answers in ways similar to the following.) Yes, they wash themselves with their tongues. Do you lick yourself to get clean? Maybe when you get something on your fingers, you lick them. Have you ever done that? What does your mother say about that? She tells you to use a napkin, doesn't she? Or she wants you to eat with your fork and spoon. We may especially lick our fingers after we've eaten fried chicken, but we don't normally clean ourselves that way. Animals are made differently from us. How many animals have you seen wearing thermal underwear? Or winter coats? We have three ducks in our backyard, and they've been out there all winter long. The only thing they have for protection is their little lean-to, a little shelter for them to go into to get out of the snow, which they don't like very much. When it was twenty degrees below zero, we gave them water a couple of times a day, and they were fine. You and I couldn't live out there without good warm clothes on. No sir! Even if we had good warm clothes on, we couldn't stay out there day after day after day.

God planned things that are good for us and things that are good for cats and things that are good for dogs. He's provided all of these special things, even if we do think some of them are different and weird, for us to enjoy and take care of. That means we need to take care of the animals and help all of God's creation to get along well, rather than try to disturb them. Sometimes we don't know how to take care of an animal, or maybe we don't know how to help a friend. Then we should ask God to give us wisdom and show us what we can do to help.

If you ever see a cat carrying its baby, don't worry; she's not eating the baby. She's moving it to a safer place. Just leave her alone. She'll be okay. Sometimes we need to remember to leave the things of nature alone, because they'll do much better if we don't mess around with them. Let's join together in prayer to thank God for all the animals he has given to us.

PRAYER: We thank you, God, for making animals and human beings so different. We thank you for loving all of the things that you have created. The Bible tells us that you looked at what you created and said that it was all good. Help us to be wise as we grow up and learn how to take care of animals and insects and trees and plants. Thank you, Lord, for all of the wonderful things you have given to us. Amen.

THERE ARE MANY EXCITING STORIES IN THE BIBLE

MYSTERY BOX OBJECT: a storybook and a pencil.

THEME: The Bible is packed full of wonderful stories. Stories for all ages. Stories that should be read every day. Stories that are full of truth.

SCRIPTURE: Fix these words of mine in your hearts and minds; tie them as symbols on your hands and bind them on your foreheads. Teach them to your children, talking about them when you sit at home and when you walk along the road, when you lie down and when you get up. Write them on the doorframes of your houses and on your gates, so that your days and the days of your children may be many in the land that the LORD swore to give your forefathers, as many as the days that the heavens are above the earth. (Deuteronomy 11:18-21)

LESSON:

Let's see what we have in the mystery box today. I see two things in here today. There's a book and a pencil.

Well, I have some questions for you. What are books good for? How many of you read books? I bet you don't even like to read books. Books aren't any good. Oh, you think books are good? Sure they are. We learn things from the stories inside. Raise your hand if you read a book or if someone read you part of a book yesterday. Books are *super* things. There's so much to learn from books.

As we grow older, the kinds of books we like are different. The stories you read now and enjoy will be different from the stories you will read when you get older. Sometimes your mom and dad may read to you, and some of you are even old enough to read on your own. Books can become very special friends.

What good are pencils? You shouldn't write in your reading books. Pencils are good for writing things on paper or in notebooks. Reading books are to read and are not to be written in.

Did you know that God has a book? We call it the Bible. Some of it is pretty hard for children to read, but your mom or dad can read portions of the Bible to you and help you understand it. There are so many interesting stories in the Bible for everyone—the very youngest to the very oldest. The Bible is God's book—a very important book.

I am sure that this book I had in the mystery box will be read by someone somewhere today, and whoever listens to it will enjoy it. I want you all to ask your moms and dads to read you a story from the Bible today, or you might read it all by yourself. When you are all done reading, you can take a pencil and rewrite the story in your own words on a piece of paper.

PRAYER: Thank you, Father, that your book has so many wonderful stories in it. Help us to remember to read it every day. Amen.

GOD GIVES US GOOD THINGS

MYSTERY BOX OBJECT: a roll of toilet paper.

THEME: God created everything. We need to take care of all the good things he gives us.

SCRIPTURE: In the beginning was the Word, and the Word was with God, and the Word was God. He was with God in the beginning. Through him all things were made; without him nothing was made that has been made. (John 1:1-3)

LESSON:

If you want to see what's in the box, just come up here, and look inside. I'm going to shake it. It doesn't rattle, and it's very light. I don't know if I should be worried or not. It rolls around a little when I move the box. Let's take a look and see what's inside.

This has got to be the best yet. I'll pull it out and try not to be too embarrassed. How many of you have this kind of stuff at your house? It comes in pretty handy at times, doesn't it? Some of you are laughing. Well, we can laugh at toilet paper, but it is important around the house.

There are a lot of useful things around the house. Did you know that toilet paper comes from wood? Now how would you like to have a log hanging up in your bathroom? No way! Where does wood come from? God gave us wood by making trees. All the things in our homes, including toilet paper, come from things that God has given us, and God gave us minds so that we can use the things he has provided to make our lives better.

We don't have logs hanging in our bathrooms, we have paper. That's because there are people in factories who know how to "chew" the wood into very fine bits and make soft paper. Then it becomes useful to us. The clothes you are wearing are not made of paper. Some clothes are made of cotton, which grows on small bushes. People pick the cotton and send it to a factory, where it goes through special processing. When the processing is done, we are able to make clothes with it.

Some of our clothes are made of wool, which comes from sheep. Sheep have something like fur on them, and sheep farmers give the sheep a haircut and shear the wool. Someone else takes the wool to a factory to spin it and make it into yarn for knitting clothes. Some of our clothes are made from synthetic fibers, which are made from plastics and chemicals.

The Bible tells us that God created everything that we see and know. The next time you go to the bathroom and tear off a few sheets of toilet paper, I want you to think about where it comes from. I don't want you to think only about the fact that we are able to go to the store and buy the paper, but that God gave us the wood in the trees to make the paper. God has given us all that we have, so we are able to live as well as we do.

We should never waste anything that God has given us. You shouldn't throw paper around just for the fun of it. All of us should take care of everything in our world. A person once told me, "If you can't make it, then don't destroy it.'' That's a good motto for all of us to live by. We shouldn't destroy things that we can't make, and we need to trust God to give us the ability to take care of the special things he has given to us.

PRAYER: Father, we thank you for all that you have given us. We thank you for special things, like toilet paper, that you provide. Help us to remember this week to take care of all the good things you have given to us. Amen.

PRAYER: TALKING TO GOD

MYSTERY BOX OBJECT: a walkie-talkie.

THEME: God wants us to talk to him.

SCRIPTURE: Then Jesus told his disciples a parable to show them that they should always pray and not give up. (Luke -18:1)

LESSON:

How many of you have walkie-talkies? How many of you have ever played with them? Walkie-talkies are fun, but what can you do with them? (Respond to answers in a way similar to what follows.) Okay, you can talk to other people. Do you ever say anything important? Sometimes you might have to. Walkie-talkies are like telephones, but you don't have to dial a number to talk to someone. The other person has to have a walkie-talkie, and must have it turned on to hear you.

How many of you know how to use a telephone? Telephones are easy and fun to use. We can send all kinds of messages over the telephone. What kind of message would you send? What do you tell people when you talk on the phone? Have you ever told anyone over the telephone that you love him or her? Perhaps a grandparent or an aunt or uncle or someone far away? Have you ever yelled at someone over the telephone? I bet you'd like that! The person can't smack you or do anything to you. Have you ever talked to someone about television over the telephone? Maybe a special program that you liked? How about your toys? Or have you ever told someone about what's happening to you or about someone you know? Maybe you can talk to someone in another state and compare the weather in your states. You can talk about all kinds of things on telephones and on walkie-talkies.

You can do the same thing with God! Do you think he wants to listen to what you have to say? He wants to hear all the things that you might say to someone on the telephone—and more! He wants to hear about the times you fall down and scrape your knee. He wants to hear about the things you like and the things you don't like. He wants to hear about how miserable or how good you think the weather is. Talking to God is like talking on a walkie-talkie. With a walkie-talkie, you can go wherever you want and be heard by the person on the other end.

Talking to God is like that. Wherever you go or whatever you do, he's always on the other end of the walkie-talkie. God can always hear you, even if you whisper, and he can even hear you think! He always is listening, and he answers back. Sometimes, he talks to us through other people, sometimes in our thoughts, sometimes when we read the Bible, and many times things happen that we know can only come from God.

I know you must have a lot of fun with walkie-talkies when you play. Prayer can be a lot of fun, too, when you know that the person on the other end loves you and cares about what happens to you. Let's talk to God—we don't need a walkie-talkie. While I'm talking, you can talk in your own mind. You don't even have to say words. All you have to do is think in your minds what you want to say to God. He knows. He can hear you. He understands.

PRAYER: God, we thank you that we don't have to wait for you to answer the telephone. We thank you that we don't have to wait for you to pick up the other end of a walkie-talkie to hear what we have to say to you. You are always there, and you are always ready to listen and hear us and let us know that you love us. Help us to know that our prayers don't have to be in fancy words, but if we talk to you just as we do on a telephone or a walkie-talkie about things that really concern us, you'll hear us. Father, take all of these young people and hear what they are saying to you, not only now but all the time, and answer their prayers. Let them know you are just as close, even closer, than the person at the other end of a walkie-talkie. Amen.

LOVE

MYSTERY BOX OBJECT: a figure holding a heart placard that reads, "This is how much I love you."

THEME: We need to tell our friends and family that we love them.

SCRIPTURE: My command is this: Love each other as I have loved you. Greater love has no one than this, that he lay down his life for his friends. (John 15:12-13)

LESSON:

Look at this funny little guy who has a red heart that says, "This is how much I love you." Do any of you have a little red heart that sticks out like this one? I can't see the heart that is inside of you, and you can't see mine. What does your heart do inside your body? It beats in your chest. It sounds like a little drum. Your heart pumps blood through your body. If your heart were to stop beating, you would die. All the doctors and nurses who go to church here would run down here to help you, and everyone would be screaming and yelling. But that's not going to happen because your heart is beating and circulating the blood through your body, and that gives you life.

This figure is holding a heart that says, "I love you this much." Do you love anyone that much? Yes, we love a lot of people that much. The important question is this: Have you ever told someone that you love him or her that much? If you love someone, that's great, that's super, but if you never tell that person that you love him or her, then just think how sad that person would be never knowing you love her or him so much.

A friend of mine told me a story. He was walking down the street and saw a friend of his. He stopped and talked with his friend, then turned and went home. It was only one-half hour later that my friend received a phone call and was told that the person he had stopped to talk to on the street had died. My friend told me, "You know, I have no regrets because I always try to tell everyone exactly what he or she means to me all the time. If anything ever happens to them, then nothing is left unsaid." What that says to us is that we should tell the people around us that we care about them.

It's always important to say the words *I love you,* and there are many ways to say it. When your mom puts a good meal on the table or when you get up in the morning and have nice, fresh, clean clothes to wear, do you ever say "thank you"? That's another way of saying "I love you. I've noticed what you have done for me." When something gets broken, and you take it to your dad, do you thank him for fixing it?

How many of you have said "I love you" to your brother or sister this past week? (Respond to answers.) Now, let's be honest. Sometimes brothers and sisters don't agree with us and maybe even fight with us. But it's better to say "I love you" and try to work out the problem than to fight about it.

A hug and a kiss are good ways to say "I love you." Every night before I went to bed I used to hug my mom and dad. I'd do the same before I went to school in the mornings. Now when my mom and dad come to visit or when we go to visit them, the first thing we do is hug each other. By that hug, we say "I love you."

This week I want each of you to tell all the people in your house that you love them. You may do it by thanking them for something they have done for you or by hugging them or by a kiss. That will be a good challenge for all of us. Let's ask God to help us do that this week.

PRAYER: Father, we want to thank you for love. We want to tell you that we love you and that we are really glad that you love us. Help us to show more love to those around us in our homes and at school and when we play. Sometimes it's hard to say, "I love you," and sometimes we don't know how to show people that we love them. Remind us this week to show our love to the people in our family and to our friends and to you. In Jesus' name we pray. Amen.

GOD WANTS US TO TAKE CARE OF EACH OTHER

MYSTERY BOX OBJECT: a stuffed toy dog.

THEME: We need to take care of each other and our pets.

SCRIPTURE: My purpose is that they may be encouraged in heart and united in love. (Colossians 2:2*a*)

LESSON:

There's something heavy in the box this week. Isn't this a cute little dog? How many of you have dogs at home? How many of you have another kind of pet at home? (Respond to answers.) No one at our house really likes to take care of pets. So all we have are three smelly ducks and a fish. Fish don't take much care, do they?

How many of you have to take care of your pet? Usually pets need to be taken care of and that takes a lot of work. Anything that's alive needs our help.

A pet requires food and water. When it's hot, a pet needs a lot of water. We should never keep our pets in a car for long periods of time, and we should make sure our pets get lots of exercise.

The plants at home need care, too. Everything needs somebody to care for it. Did you know that we are a lot like that? Most of us need someone to take care of us and to care about us.

How many of you do everything for yourselves? Do you get your own breakfast, lunch, and dinner? Do you wash your own clothes? Do you clean your own room? (Respond to answers.) I can see now that you are thinking that there is not one of us here that does everything by himself or herself. Not one of us. We all need help once in a while. Isn't it wonderful that God made families to take care of each other? If I need help with something at my house, all I have to do is ask someone to help me. Now I don't always get the help exactly when I want it, but usually I do. And when someone at my house needs help, I try to help the best way I can.

This toy dog doesn't need any food. You don't have to feed it or give it water, but it's still a nice pet. Real pets need a lot of help, and so do people. It's really nice when we are willing to help each other. God wants us to be willing to help when we can. Sometimes we should help each other without being asked. When we help each other without being asked to help, we do it because we love each other.

We love our pets and take good care of them, and we need to take care of each other, too. God takes care of us and loves us. Let's ask God to help us to help each other willingly and lovingly.

PRAYER: Lord, when you look at us, you see that some of us are weak and need help in a lot of areas. We thank you for those around us who can help. We thank you for the love we share together. Most of all we pray that you will continue to help each one of us to grow physically, so that we can be big and strong. Help us to learn more about your Son, Jesus, and to trust him. Bless us with that special help today. Amen.

GOD MADE EACH OF US DIFFERENT

MYSTERY BOX OBJECT: a drinking cup.

THEME: We're glad that God made us different. Each one of us is special to God.

SCRIPTURE: Now you are the body of Christ, and each one of you is a part of it. (I Corinthians 12:27)

LESSON:

How many of you drink out of cups and glasses at home? How many of you don't use cups? How would you drink a cup of hot tea? Would you use your hands? No way! That would burn your hands. So you would put the tea in a cup. If you used your hands to drink something cold, it might feel good on your hands, but it would run through your fingers, wouldn't it? So someone invented the cup. That was a good idea, wasn't it? You can put hot stuff in a cup, and you can put cold stuff in a cup as well.

If there was no such thing as a cup, do you think you might have invented it? I think any of you could have done it. Do you think an elephant could have invented the cup? No. What's the difference between you and an elephant? Besides the fact that elephants are big and gray and have a trunk and a tail, what makes them different from you? (Respond to answers.) Why is it that we can invent things and an elephant can't? (Respond to answers.) That's right, elephants don't have hands. They don't live in houses either. I'm thinking more of what goes on up here, in my head. God gave elephants and other animals one kind of brain and people another kind of brain. I'm going to try and think like an elephant. It wakes up in the morning and thinks, ''I'm thirsty.'' Then it looks around for water. After getting a drink it thinks, ''I'm hungry.'' Then the elephant looks around for trees or plants to grab with its trunk and eat. Do you know that elephants don't go to work? They don't play baseball, and in the winter they don't go skiing. We're different from animals because God has given us a brain to think of all the things that need to be done. He also gave us a brain to think of ways to make things better. Now an elephant would never think about digging a ditch and piping water in from a nearby river. An elephant would never think about planting a garden so it would have a lot to eat. We do think about things like that!

Someone invented the cup so we don't have to drink with our hands. Do you want to go down to the river and put your head in the water to get a drink? No way! God his given us a special brain so we can think about doing things, unlike any other creature on earth. What I'm trying to tell you is that you are someone special! Even though we all have a brain, none of us can think alike. If I gave each of you a piece of clay and told you to make a cup, without telling you what a cup looks like, everyone would make something different. In school when the art teacher tells you to draw something, your picture is always different from everyone else's. That's because God has made you different from anyone else. God made you special! I wouldn't want to be anyone else but myself! I'm happy just being me! Are you happy being you? You should be, because there is no one else just like you. I'm happy you are you. Let's thank God for cups, but let's thank him more for making each of us different and very special in his eyes.

PRAYER: Lord, we thank you that someone invented a cup, so we don't have to drink out of our hands. Lord, we thank you even more that you gave each one of us a brain. We're glad you made each of us different. Each of us is special to you. We think differently and dress differently and wear our hair differently, but you love us all the same. We love you, too, Jesus and give you all the praise. Amen.

JESUS MAKES US BEAUTIFUL INSIDE

MYSTERY BOX OBJECT: a bubble blower.

THEME: When we let Jesus into our lives, he helps us to become angels of mercy to those who are sad or feeling bad.

SCRIPTURE: We have different gifts, according to the grace given us . . . if it is encouraging, let him encourage; if it is contributing to the needs of others, let him give generously. (Romans 12:6*a*, 8*a*)

LESSON:

Let's see what we have in the box today. It feels light. I don't think it's very big. Let's take a look. It's a bubble blower. What do you do with this thing? Blow bubbles? I'm going to blow into it, and we can see what kind of bubbles it makes. It doesn't work! Why won't it work? I need to put soap into it to make bubbles come out? I see. We can't use it for anything the way it is, can we?

How many of you have ever had a bubble blower before? They have been around for many years. I had one when I was a boy. It wasn't quite like this one. This one is a fancy one. It makes a lot of bubbles, doesn't it? They are pretty nifty things. All we have to do is dip the blower into the liquid soap, shake it through the air, and we get bubbles! But as long as we don't have any soap, it isn't any good.

Did you know that some of us are like this bubble blower? Yes, we are! If the right ingredients are added to our lives, we can do some pretty terrific things. Without these special things, we're really not worth much. Of course, we're talking about Jesus. Without Jesus in our lives, we are a lot like one of these little bubble blowers—without soap, no bubbles!

Some of us go through our whole lives never doing anything really important. Until we are willing to give ourselves to Jesus and let him flow into our lives, just like the soap flows into the bubble blower, nothing will happen. When we wave the bubble blower through the air and the wind catches it, we get beautiful bubbles. In the same way, if you let Jesus into your life, learn about him, follow what he teaches in the Bible, then you can do some beautiful things in the world. The people around you will look at your life, and they'll see Jesus in your life. You won't be just an empty person, bouncing around through the world, but you'll be someone very beautiful and very special.

How many of you want to be someone very beautiful for Jesus? I'm not talking about the way you look on the outside, but about how Jesus can change you on the inside and make you special. Would you like to look like an angel? Sometimes you and I become angels of mercy for someone who is sad or feeling bad. Without Jesus, we can't be the angels of mercy he wants us to be. We need Jesus in our hearts.

Let's pray together and ask Jesus to take our lives and make something very beautiful with them.

PRAYER: Lord, when I look at all these children, I think they are so beautiful. I pray that you will take their lives and, through their moms and dads and the people of this church, help them to know more about Jesus so that they can be something beautiful for you. When people see the things they do and hear the things they say, they will see only you and give you the honor. Father, help us to open our lives so you can come in. We pray in the name of the One who makes us beautiful: Jesus himself. Amen.

CHRISTIANS HAVE LOTS OF FUN

MYSTERY BOX OBJECT: sewing cards.

THEME: We can be Christians and still have a good time.

SCRIPTURE: In addition to our own encouragement, we were especially delighted to see how happy Titus was, because his spirit has been refreshed by all of you. (II Corinthians 7:13)

LESSON:

Look at this! I've got some sewing cards. What are they used for? Do you use them to hit your sister or brother? No, they are for learning. The long string goes into one hole and out the other and then into another hole and out another.

There are many toys that help us to learn. Toys aren't just something to play with; many toys teach something to us.

When I was a kid, my cousin had the neatest toy. It was a scale. We use a scale to weigh things. Her scale had numbers of different sizes. If she put the numbers one and two on one side of the scale, then she had to pick number three for the other side in order to balance it out. She learned her numbers and how to count that way.

Sometimes toys are for fun, and sometimes they teach us different things. That's why we have the mystery box. You have fun bringing in something you like, and then we learn from it. By using the mystery box, you become a part of what happens in our church service each Sunday. We don't just do adult things in our service; church is for people of all ages. We want you to have fun in church, and, at the same time, we want you to learn about Jesus. It's important to remember as you grow older that we can be good Christians and still laugh and have a good time.

Let's have a word of prayer and thank the Lord for allowing us to have a good time.

PRAYER: Father, we thank you for allowing us to have a good time here in church. We thank you for allowing us to learn about you and to have fun and be able to laugh at ourselves and talk about things that are important to us. Help us all, Lord, not just the young, but those of us who are older as well, to know that being a Christian doesn't mean that we have to frown all the time. We can laugh and have a good time. We pray in your Son's name. Amen.

WORKING TOGETHER, HELPING EACH OTHER

MYSTERY BOX OBJECT: baseball cards.

THEME: Everyone has a job to do.

SCRIPTURE: Lazy hands make a man poor, but diligent hands bring wealth. (Proverbs 10:4)

LESSON:

I love what we have in the mystery box today! Baseball cards! What do you do with these cards? (Respond to answers in ways similar to what follows.) Okay, you can look at them. What do you have to do to get your picture on one of these cards? How many of you play in Little League? Do you have your picture on a card? You don't? Why not? You don't think you are good enough? I don't know about that! You aren't old enough, that's for sure. All of these fellows are what we call professionals.

Your mom and dad get up early in the morning and get ready to work. The baseball players on these cards get up early in the morning and play baseball. It's not something they do for fun. They may have fun playing baseball, but it is still their job.

Everyone has a job. What is your job? Both of my sons have jobs. One has to feed the ducks, and the other has to feed the fish. Feeding the fish is not a hard job, but the fish would die if it didn't get food, so that is an important job.

Do you ever make your bed at home? Do you ever hang up your clothes or put toys away or help to set the table? All of these are important jobs. They are just as important as feeding the fish.

There are jobs that need to be done around the house, and there are jobs that need to be done around the church. Can you think of jobs that need to be done around the church? (*Respond to answers in ways similar to what follows.*) Yes, someone has to buy flowers for each Sunday. The flower committee takes care of that job. Someone has to type up the bulletin each week, and that's another job. The ushers have the job of handing out the bulletins and taking the offering. Then at the end of the service the greeters are always at the door, waiting to shake our hands. Some jobs that you might do at your age are picking up papers around the church and making sure there is no chewing gum under the seats and not running in church. Coming to Sunday school and church to learn about Jesus is a very important job! As you get older, more jobs will be available to you. Your job may not be as flashy as playing baseball and having your picture on a card, but God will know what you have done, and that's much more important.

So, when you get older and there are jobs that need to be done around the church, remember that it's important to help. If you don't do these jobs, who will? We have to start training you early, so in a couple of years you will be ushers and greeters and committee members and Sunday school teachers, helping to take care of this church.

PRAYER: Lord, we thank you for these children. Help them as they grow older to understand that all the jobs they do are very important, but none so important as working in your church. Help us all to do better at the jobs we do every day. Amen.

WE ARE GOD'S MOST IMPORTANT CREATION

MYSTERY BOX OBJECT: shaped blocks.

THEME: The Bible tells us that, of all the shapes God made, of all the things God created, the most important thing he created was us.

SCRIPTURE: So God created man in his own image, in the image of God he created him; male and female he created them. (Genesis 1:27)
For God so loved the world that he gave his one and only Son, that whoever believes in him shall not perish but have eternal life. (John 3:16)

LESSON:

Does anyone know what this is? It's a _____ (tell what the shape is) block. There are a lot of different shapes in the world. We don't take enough time to stop and look at all the different shapes that God has created for us.

What shape is a tree? (Respond to answers.) If you were to cut through the trunk of a tree, the trunk would be in the shape of a circle. If you stand in front of a tree, you'll see that it is tall. If you've ever had the opportunity to look at a tree from above, you know that it looks like a big green round spot on the ground. All the leaves on the tree have different shapes, and the leaves of each kind of tree are shaped differently from all other kinds of trees.

What shape are a mom and a dad? A person shape! Yes, moms and dads come in different sizes and shapes.

God has made many different sizes and shapes of things, and, like this block, it depends on how we turn them as to what we see. God created everything that we can see. We are all different. Some of us have round faces, and some of us have long thin faces. The Bible tells us that of all the shapes in the world, of all the things God has created, the most important shape God created is us!

He loves everyone of us. No matter where we are, what we look like, or how we act, he still loves us. Sometimes, we are like this block. When we are turned a certain way, we're happy. But if we are turned another way, we are sad. If we are turned yet another way, we get angry or upset. The most important thing we have to offer God is ourselves. We need to remember that God loves us all the time, and he wants us to come to him, no matter how different we think we are.

PRAYER: God, thank you for loving us, even though we all come in different sizes and shapes. Bless all of us today, not just the little ones, but the bigger ones as well. Help us to know you love us. In Jesus' name we pray. Amen.

KNOWING RIGHT FROM WRONG

MYSTERY BOX OBJECT: a superhero toy figure.

THEME: The Bible tells us what is right and what is wrong.

SCRIPTURE: As for me, far be it from me that I should sin against the LORD by failing to pray for you. And I will teach you the way that is good and right. (I Samuel 12:23)

LESSON:

I know who this guy is. This is _____ (name the character). He's a character on a TV cartoon. He isn't a real person. He's just a cartoon character who fights cartoon bad guys.

Sometimes in our lives, we are faced with a decision between something that is good and something that is bad. Sometimes we are faced with an even harder decision, and that is choosing between two things that are good.

What do you think God would want you to choose, the good or the bad? (Respond to answers.) Yes, God always wants us to choose the good. If I were to tell you to walk quietly downstairs, or if I said you could run downstairs screaming and yelling and throwing things at one another, which would you choose? (Respond to answers.) Good, you would choose to walk quietly. Why? You have been taught that you shouldn't run around and be loud and throw things in the church building, God's house. Most of you know what is good and bad, what is right and wrong, because you have been told. Moms and dads teach us right from wrong, and so does the Bible. No matter how old you are, you will have to choose between good and bad.

_____ (name the character) always chooses the good. We should always choose the good because that is what God wants us to do. When you choose the bad, you usually feel bad, especially if you get punished for what you did. The reason for punishment is to help you to learn and understand and remember what is good and what is bad. Bad things bring bad things to you, but good things bring good things to you.

Let's thank God for giving us the opportunity to choose good things.

PRAYER: Lord, we want to thank you for moms and dads and other people who help us understand what is right from wrong. For some of us that is hard because we're still small. Help us to choose good always. Help us to learn from our parents and other adults the good things you want us to do and to know. In Jesus' name we pray. Amen.

WE DON'T WANT TO BE STRANGERS TO GOD

MYSTERY BOX OBJECT: a toy hippopotamus.

THEME: God wants us to know him and be his close friend.

SCRIPTURE: For God did not send his Son into the world to condemn the world, but to save the world through him. (John 3:17)

LESSON:

A hippopotamus is a very big animal. I'm sure you have seen a picture of one, or maybe you have even seen one at the zoo. But no hippos live in the woods around here, do they? I haven't seen any. Hippos live in Africa, where it's warm and wet. They don't like the cold weather we have here.

Do you like the water? Hippos live in the water. How many of you eat grass? Nobody eats grass! But that's what a hippo eats.

We're different from hippos, and we're different from one another. How many of you like pizza? How many of you like liver and onions? How many of you like hamburgers? I see that some of you like hamburgers and pizza and liver and onions, and some of you don't. We look and talk differently from one another.

One thing we all have in common is that we are far away from God. God wants us to be very close to him. All of us are strangers to God if we haven't asked him to be a part of our lives. He wants us to do that. When we have God in our lives, we become friends with him and do what he wants us to do. God is continually working with us, getting us to change for the better.

We always have more fun with our friends than with strangers. When we meet someone who is a stranger to us, we work at being friends with that person, and soon we are having fun, too. God wants you to know him well and get close to him and like him a lot. He wants you to know that he will always take care of you and be your best friend. Let's pray to our special friend.

PRAYER: Heavenly Father, we thank you for making each one of us different. We thank you that we all look different and talk differently and act differently, and we even like different kinds of food. We thank you for making us that way. Thank you, God, for wanting to be our friend, and we want to be friends with you. Help us not to be strangers anymore, and teach us to be your friend forever. In your Son's name, we pray. Amen.

WE NEED TO LEARN TO WAIT QUIETLY

MYSTERY BOX OBJECT: a picture of a baby.

THEME: God provides good things for those who wait.

SCRIPTURE:
> Yet the LORD longs to be gracious to you;
> he rises to show you compassion.
> For the LORD is a God of justice.
> Blessed are all who wait for him! (Isaiah 30:18)

LESSON:

This is a picture of a baby. (If you know the baby, say something about him or her and about the parents.) Like all parents, this baby's mom and dad anxiously awaited the birth of their child. They looked forward to their child's arrival.

How many of you have ever looked forward to something special, like Christmas or Halloween or your birthday?

We always have to wait, don't we? Does your mom or dad say, "No, not now. Maybe later," or "Next week"? You don't like to hear that. What's even worse is their telling you that you can do something "on your next birthday." That always seems like such a long time to wait.

God tells us in the Bible that we have to wait for good things to come our way. Sometimes waiting makes whatever happens even better. What if every day was Christmas Day? Now that sounds pretty good, doesn't it? But if every day were Christmas Day, all the excitement would be gone. It would be like getting up and eating cereal every morning—no big deal! But Christmas comes only once a year, and that makes it exciting.

How many of you have prayed to God for something, but didn't get it right away? I've prayed many times for something special and have had to wait for an answer. God tells us we need to wait quietly and listen to him speak to us when we pray. Sometimes we have to wait for an answer to our prayers; sometimes he says yes right away; and sometimes he says no right away. But he always listens to us, and he always answers our prayers, sooner or later.

Next time you ask God for something, think about the fact that you may not get an answer right away. Give God time, because as you learn to wait, he is going to provide the very best things for you.

PRAYER: God, we thank you for giving us this time together. We thank you for always giving us your very best. You have promised to give us good things if we wait patiently. Help us to wait. We thank you that you listen to our prayers no matter how old we are. Amen.

GOD NEVER MAKES MISTAKES

MYSTERY BOX OBJECT: a snow dome.

THEME: It is no accident that it snows in winter.

SCRIPTURE: He causes his sun to rise on the evil and the good, and sends rain on the righteous and the unrighteous. (Matthew 5:45*b*)

LESSON:

What is this? Isn't it pretty! It has water inside, and when I shake it, it looks like it is snowing inside.

How many of you like snow? Would you like it to snow in July? Would you like eighty-degree weather for Christmas? Some places have warm weather during Christmas. We don't have warm weather here in December, and we don't have snow in July. It wouldn't be good for the gardens. The seasons change for a reason. Some would give us a scientific reason why it snows in the winter and is eighty degrees in the summer. But it makes more sense to say we have snow in the winter because God made it that way.

It's no accident that we all look different. It's no accident that some of you were born in this town, and some of you were born many miles from here. It's no accident that you were born into your family. With God there are no accidents, because he does everything according to a special plan. It's no accident that you are here with me on this Sunday. You all look so nice today. I like being with you, and I want to thank you for coming to church today. Being here together and sharing the mystery box this morning is no accident. It's nice to be here together, isn't it?

I want you to remember when you see snow or when you see sunshine or when you see someone who looks different from you that it is not an accident. That's how God wants it.

PRAYER: Lord, we don't have palms to wave this morning as the people did for Jesus so many years ago. But we want to thank you for being here with us this morning. Help us to know your love. Amen.

GOD LOVES US SO MUCH THAT HE SENT HIS SON

MYSTERY BOX OBJECT: magnet figures of people.

THEME: God touches our lives in a special way to let us know that he loves us.

SCRIPTURE: This is how we know what love is: Jesus Christ laid down his life for us. And we ought to lay down our lives for our brothers. (I John 3:16)

LESSON:

Have you ever seen two people putting their faces together like this before? (Put two of the magnets together as if they are kissing.) Of course, you have, when two people kiss. How many of you have ever kissed anyone? There is nothing wrong with kissing. I bet you kiss your mom and dad when you go to bed at night. Many people kiss each other goodbye when they go somewhere. Maybe you do that, too. I'm sure you kiss your grandparents. It's never ''sissy'' for children to kiss their parents. Kissing is a special way of telling people that you like them.

We can't kiss God. God is a Spirit. God is always with us, and he touches our lives in special ways to let us know he loves us. Sometimes I would like to be able to kiss God, but I can't. I just tell him how much I love him. God loves you and me so much that he let his only Son die for us. That's real love!

We need to trust in God. He knows when we need something, and he always takes care of that need. That's God's way of saying, ''I love you.'' God doesn't kiss us the way our moms and dads do, but we need to know that God loves us more than we will ever understand.

I want you to remember to kiss someone special this week. By doing that, you will be saying, ''I love you.'' Remember to tell God you love him, too.

PRAYER: Lord, we thank you that you love us so much that you gave us your Son. We want you to know that we love you very much. Amen.

GOD NEVER WANTS US TO BE SELF-CENTERED

MYSTERY BOX OBJECT: Dr. Seuss's *Cat in the Hat.*

THEME: Jesus said he would like us to do the same to other people that he has done for us.

SCRIPTURE: Do not be misled. "Bad company corrupts good character." (I Corinthians 15:33)

LESSON:

Everyone knows the story of *The Cat in the Hat.* The cat causes a lot of mischief, doesn't he? What does he do to get himself into trouble? (Respond to answers.) He makes a mess of other people's homes. Do you go to someone's house and make a mess? If you do, do you help to clean it up? I don't know exactly what the cat in the hat's problem is, but sometimes he just doesn't think of others. He thinks only of himself. He is self-centered.

Sometimes we think only of ourselves, and we forget about everyone else. We do what we want no matter what the people around us think. We think, "It's my life, and I'll do what I want." But we don't stop to think of how our behavior affects those around us. Does that happen to you? I think that each one of us is guilty of thinking only of what he or she wants and not about what other people need or want.

God never does that. God is never self-centered. He never thinks only of himself and forgets about us. In fact, God has always done just the opposite. God always thinks about us first. He cares about us and wants the very best for us. Unlike the cat in this book, God is always there to do something for us. God cares so much for us that he sent his only Son, Jesus, to earth to die on the cross, so that we could ask forgiveness and have a clean heart and learn from him. He let his Son come to earth and die so that you and I could have eternal life. Do you think that we love one another so much we would be willing to do that? The cat in this book probably wouldn't go out of his way to do anything for anyone.

Jesus said that he'd like us to do the same for other people that he has done for us. This means—and this is the tough part—that when your mom or dad asks you to do something, you should do it without complaining or whining or crying. We all have done that at some time or another. Of course, that's part of growing up, but God wants us to learn, as we grow up, to be like Jesus, not like the cat in the hat. We need to learn to think about other people and care about what happens to them more than we care about what happens to ourselves. That is a difficult lesson to learn, but with Jesus' help, we can do it.

You can start by trying to help other people when they need it. If someone falls down, don't laugh, go to the person and find out whether he or she needs help. Instead of complaining to your mom and dad all the time, try not complaining and learn to say, "Okay, I'll do what you want." Put a smile on your face and get to work. That's what Jesus wants us to do.

The cat is not a bad guy to read about, but I wouldn't want him for a friend, would you? Jesus is the kind of person I like for a friend.

PRAYER: Heavenly Father, thank you for sending us your Son. We're glad that he isn't like the cat in the hat. Your Son is loving and cares about us and shows us how to care for others. Help us to learn to live that way, too. Amen.

GOD WILL NEVER MAKE FUN OF YOU

MYSTERY BOX OBJECT: a very strange looking toy creature.

THEME: God made us the way we are. We all look different on the outside, but God wants us to look the same on the inside with a clean heart.

SCRIPTURE: The body is a unit, though it is made up of many parts; and though all its parts are many, they form one body. So it is with Christ. For we were all baptized by one Spirit into one body. (I Corinthians 12:12-13*a*)

LESSON:

This is a friend of mine. You think that's funny? This is a very strange looking creature, don't you agree?

We're all strange in our own way. Some of us look funny; some of us act funny; some of us think we're funny. We're all different. Take just a few minutes to look around this room and look at all the people sitting here. Take a good look! Some have light hair; some have dark hair; some have big noses; some have little noses. God made us the way we are on purpose. He made each of us different on the outside, and that makes us special.

I want you to think carefully for a while. Has anyone ever made fun of you? Have you ever heard someone making fun of another person? Have you ever made fun of anyone? Sometimes that happens. When I was in the first grade, I had to wear glasses for the first time. As I remember it, I was the only one in the entire school who wore glasses. All the other kids called me "four-eyes." I was shy then, and that really hurt me. I'll never forget one place I could go and not be made fun of. That place was my Sunday school class. My friends from Sunday school never called me "four-eyes." They accepted me the way I was. That helped me to understand that God would never make fun of me either and that he loved me just the way I was, whether I wore glasses or not.

That's how God wants us to be. The Bible tells us that God loves every human being. He loves children as much as he loves adults. God doesn't care about how we look on the outside, but he cares very much what we look like on the inside. He wants us to have a clean heart. With a clean heart, we will try never to make fun of anyone who looks different on the outside.

I want you to think about that the next time you hear someone making fun of another person, or even if you are tempted to make fun of someone. Remember that God would never do that. Instead, he wraps his arms of love around us.

PRAYER: Father, thank you that no matter how I look, you still love me. I thank you for the people you have given me who surround me with their love. Reveal yourself to these young people and help them to understand how important it is to have a clean heart, because that's what you care most about. In Jesus' name we pray. Amen.

A STRONG HEART—PHYSICALLY
AND SPIRITUALLY

MYSTERY BOX OBJECT: a jump rope.

THEME: We need to exercise our spiritual body.

SCRIPTURE: Everyone who competes in the games goes into strict training. They do it to get a crown that will not last; but we do it to get a crown that will last forever. (I Corinthians 9:25)

LESSON:

Look at what we have here. There is a jump rope in the mystery box. I can jump rope! For those of you who think I can't, I'll meet you outside after the service is over.

How many of you jump rope? Jumping rope is good exercise. It helps you to develop coordination. If you jump hard enough and long enough, your heart will start pumping faster. That's good, healthy exercise for your whole body. When you get really good at it, not only can you learn to jump forward, but also you can learn to jump backwards.

I think you all look physically healthy. You are doing a lot of running and playing, and that's good. There's a part of you, though, that I can't see. That's the part called the spirit, or the soul.

We need to exercise our spiritual bodies, and we can do that by coming to church and Sunday school. We can also exercise by reading the Bible and by praying. How many of you have exercised your spiritual body this past week? (Respond to answers.)

God wants us to exercise our spiritual bodies more than we exercise our physical bodies. So use your jump rope, run, and play tag and hide-and-seek, ride your bike, and make your physical body strong and healthy. But also remember that you need to read your Bible, or have your mom or your dad read it to you. Remember to pray to God every day and come to church and Sunday school to exercise your spiritual body.

Let's do a spiritual exercise right now. Bow your heads, and as I pray, you pray too and ask God to help you remember to build up your spiritual body.

PRAYER: Lord, as you look down upon us, you see that most of us get a lot of exercise and are pretty healthy. Help us to find ways to exercise spiritually. Teach us about your Son, Jesus. Help us to read our Bibles and to find ways to talk to you, just as we are doing now. Encourage us to go to church and Sunday school. Help our parents to teach us, so that we can be strong spiritually as well as physically. We pray in the name of Jesus, the One whom we have accepted as our Lord and Savior. Amen.

GOD'S WONDERFUL CREATURES

MYSTERY BOX OBJECT: a toy horse.

THEME: God's gift to us is all his creatures, and our gift to God is to take very good care of them.

SCRIPTURE: Rule over the fish of the sea and the birds of the air and over every living creature that moves on the ground. (Genesis 1:28*b*)

LESSON:

Look at what I have! A horse! How many of you think you could ride this horse? You couldn't ride it very well, could you? You'd smash it, because this is not a real horse. How many of you have ridden a real live horse? It's a lot of fun to ride a horse. But before you get on a horse, you need to know how to ride it, so you won't get hurt.

Horses and all other farm and domestic animals need a lot of care. They need to be fed and watered. In the winter, when the snow covers all the grass, someone needs to make sure the horses get food to eat. If you had your own horse, you would learn how to brush it and how to put a saddle and a bridle on it and how to rub the horse down after you have taken it for a ride.

God has given us many wonderful animals, like horses, to enjoy. But we have to do more than just enjoy them. We must take care of them. The Bible tells us that it is our job to care for all animals, in the sea, in the air, and on the land. If we take good care of them, then we are able to enjoy them more.

How many of you have a pet at home? I am sure you take good care of your pet. You probably take your pet for a walk. Can you put a leash on your goldfish and take it for a walk? No? I guess you really can't take your goldfish for a walk. But you can feed it and make sure it has clean water. You can take your dog for a walk. You are never too young to learn how to take care of your pet.

This horse doesn't need to be fed or watered, but we need to remember that real horses and other animals do need to be taken care of.

I want you to promise me that this week you will take special care of your pet. That's what God wants you to do.

PRAYER: Father, we thank you for all the animals that you have given us for our enjoyment. Help us to remember that it is our responsibility to take care of the things you give us so that we can enjoy them more. Amen.

GOD IS THE HOLY SPIRIT—HE IS GOOD

MYSTERY BOX OBJECT: a toy ghost.

THEME: God isn't a ghost, but a Spirit. We never need to be afraid of him, because he loves us.

SCRIPTURE: The God who made the world and everything in it is the Lord of heaven and earth and does not live in temples built by hands. . . . God did this so that men would seek him and perhaps reach out for him and find him, though he is not far from each one of us. (Acts 17:24, 27)

LESSON:

I think I have an idea of what this is—it's a ghost.

How many of you have seen a ghost? (Respond to answers in ways similar to what follows.) You have? Not really, huh? I'm not going to say there is no such thing as ghosts, because sometimes in the church we talk about a ghost: the Holy Ghost. Does that sound familiar? A better definition of the word *ghost* is "spirit," and you have heard us speak of the Holy Spirit. We say that God is a Spirit. Even though there is no difference between a ghost and a spirit, we sometimes think there is.

When you think of a ghost, what do you think of? Yes, you think of a white sheeted figure that floats through the air, like Casper the friendly ghost. We think of a ghost as something that scares us. Sometimes we get scared at Halloween, but God would never scare us. God would never come in any form to scare you. If there is something that scares you, it is not from God. I can guarantee you that! God wants to give you his love. He wants us to know that we are accepted just the way we are and that he will take care of each one of us. He will never frighten us. So whenever you think about ghosts, I want you to remember that God isn't a ghost that scares us, but that God is a Spirit that loves and takes care of you.

Now, God is not like you and me. If you touch me, you will feel something solid. God has no physical form that you can grab onto and hold. It's hard sometimes to understand that. Even though we have a physical form, we are like God. He made us like himself. Another way to explain it is that your parents don't look like you, but you look like your parents. The part of you that looks like God is your spirit. Your spirit is the same as your soul, and that's the part of all of us that will live on and on after we die, if we believe in Jesus, God's Son.

Let's pray together and ask God to help us understand more about what he is like.

PRAYER: Father, I thank you that we don't have to go through life being afraid. Most of all, Father, we want to thank you that we don't have to be afraid of you. You are not the kind of God who would fill us with frightful and scary things, but rather you are the kind of God who fills us with your love. Help us to know you better, through your Son, Jesus. Bless us all, young and old. Amen.